STRATEGIC RATIONALITY IS NOT ENOUGH:
HITLER AND THE CONCEPT OF CRAZY STATES

AD-A243 579

DTIC
ELECTE
DEC 18 1991
S D

David Jablonsky

Strategic Studies Institute
U.S. Army War College

91 1217 010

SSI PROFESSIONAL READINGS IN MILITARY STRATEGY

Previous Publications

Churchill: The Making of a Grand Strategist
Colonel David Jablonsky

******

*Sun Tzu and Clausewitz: The Art of War
and On War Compared*
Dr. Michael I. Handel

******

Forthcoming

Eisenhower as Strategist
Dr. Steven Metz

******

REPORT DOCUMENTATION PAGE		Form Approved OMB No. 0704-0188

1a. REPORT SECURITY CLASSIFICATION Unclassified	1b RESTRICTIVE MARKINGS		
2a. SECURITY CLASSIFICATION AUTHORITY	3 DISTRIBUTION / AVAILABILITY OF REPORT Approved for public release; distribution unlimited		
2b. DECLASSIFICATION / DOWNGRADING SCHEDULE			
4 PERFORMING ORGANIZATION REPORT NUMBER(S) ACN 91021	5 MONITORING ORGANIZATION REPORT NUMBER(S)		

6a. NAME OF PERFORMING ORGANIZATION Strategic Studies Institute	6b. OFFICE SYMBOL (If applicable) AWCI	7a. NAME OF MONITORING ORGANIZATION
6c. ADDRESS (City, State, and ZIP Code) U.S. Army War College Carlisle Barracks, PA 17013-5050		7b. ADDRESS (City, State, and ZIP Code)
8a. NAME OF FUNDING / SPONSORING ORGANIZATION	8b. OFFICE SYMBOL (If applicable)	9 PROCUREMENT INSTRUMENT IDENTIFICATION NUMBER

8c. ADDRESS (City, State, and ZIP Code)	10. SOURCE OF FUNDING NUMBERS			
	PROGRAM ELEMENT NO	PROJECT NO.	TASK NO.	WORK UNIT ACCESSION NO

11 TITLE (Include Security Classification)

Strategic Rationality is Not Enough: Hitler and the Concept of Crazy States

12 PERSONAL AUTHOR(S)
Jablonsky, David

13a. TYPE OF REPORT Final	13b. TIME COVERED FROM _____ TO _____	14 DATE OF REPORT (Year, Month, Day) 1991 August 8	15. PAGE COUNT 111

16. SUPPLEMENTARY NOTATION

17 COSATI CODES			18. SUBJECT TERMS (Continue on reverse if necessary and identify by block number)
FIELD	GROUP	SUB-GROUP	strategy; strategic rationality; Hitler; Third Reich; crazy states

19. ABSTRACT (Continue on reverse if necessary and identify by block number)

In this report the author explores the concept on rogue or "crazy" states in the international community, an important topic in the increasingly multi-polar and dangerous world of the post-cold war era. In such an environment, the author concludes, after examining the progressive craziness of the Third Reich under Adolf Hitler, the rational basis for strategy breaks down. Strategic rationality is simply not sufficient to gauge the behavior of such states in the international arena--a particularly dangerous turn of events in an era of mass destruction weapons proliferation.

20 DISTRIBUTION / AVAILABILITY OF ABSTRACT ☒ UNCLASSIFIED/UNLIMITED ☐ SAME AS RPT ☐ DTIC USERS	21 ABSTRACT SECURITY CLASSIFICATION Unclassified	
22a. NAME OF RESPONSIBLE INDIVIDUAL Marianne P. Cowling	22b TELEPHONE (Include Area Code) (717) 245-3001	22c. OFFICE SYMBOL AWCI

DD Form 1473, JUN 86   Previous editions are obsolete.

STRATEGIC RATIONALITY IS NOT ENOUGH:
HITLER AND THE CONCEPT OF CRAZY STATES

Colonel David Jablonsky

August 8, 1991

Professional Readings in Military Strategy, No. 3

Strategic Studies Institute
U.S. Army War College
Carlisle Barracks, Pennsylvania

* * * * *

* * * * *

Comments pertaining to this publication are invited and may be forwarded to: Director, Strategic Studies Institute, U.S. Army War College, Carlisle Barracks, PA 17013-5050. Comments also may be conveyed by calling the author via commercial (717)245-3275 or AUTOVON 242-3275.

* * * * *

* * * * *

DTIC
COPY
INSPECTED
8

Accesion For	
NTIS CRA&I	✓
DTIC TAB	☐
Unannounced	☐
Justification	
By	
Distribution /	
Availability Codes	
Dist	Avail and / or Special
A-1	

CONTENTS

FIGURES

FOREWORD

The formulation of strategy at any level can normally be defined as a rational process in an instrumental sense, since the procedure involves the calculated relationship of ends and means. That calculation, in turn, includes the search for some measure of commensurability between means and ends. When that does not occur, strategists normally chose one, or a combination, of three options: increase the means, adjust the strategic concept, or change the ends.

But what if a national leader does not recognize the rational basis of strategy formulation? From a cultural or religious standpoint, for instance, what if national elites are motivated by a success through failure martyrdom outlook? Or equally important, what if leaders promote national goals that are beyond the pale in terms of humanity or sanity and set about achieving them in an instrumentally rational manner? In all these instances, as this study of the policymakers and the decision-making structure and process of Nazi Germany demonstrates, strategic rationality is not enough to gauge the behavior of such nations in the international arena. From a Western point of view, in fact, such nations are out of strategic control and have become "crazy" states.

This concept of crazy or rogue states is important for the post-cold war era, since the breakdown of the superpower bipolar nexus, although reducing East-West tensions, is also mitigating the pattern of client state stability. Historically, most rogue nations have remained isolated, local phenomena. But modern technology offers even the smallest crazy state the potential to build up significant power, particularly with weapons of mass destruction, to influence regional, if not global events. For such a dangerous, interdependent environment, there are many lessons to be drawn from the progressive radicalization of the Third Reich under Adolf Hitler.

PAUL G. CERJAN
Major General, U.S. Army
Commandant

v

CHAPTER 1

INTRODUCTION

There is an historical tendency to measure international behavior against familiar styles and norms. One reason, for example, why the threat posed by Napoleon was only gradually recognized, was that previous events, even Louis XIV's attempt at European hegemony, had accustomed policymakers to international actors who desired only to modify, not overthrow, the existing system.[1] In this century, there was a similar failure of perception in terms of the revolutionary character of Adolf Hitler and his regime. That failure, followed by the most ferocious conflict in history, has remained a cause and effect *idée fixe* for Western policymakers ever since. President Truman's intervention in Korea, for instance, was due in part to his perception of how easy it would have been to suppress Nazism in 1936 if there had been some reaction to the German remilitarization of the Rhineland. And Anthony Eden, a veteran of the diplomatic battles in the interwar years, acted in the 1956 Suez crisis on the basis of his memories of the Munich Conference and his conviction that Nassar was another Hitler.[2] Finally, there was President Johnson, rejecting a proposal to pull U.S. troops out of Vietnam, "because we learned from Hitler at Munich that success only feeds the appetite of aggression."[3]

The durability of the Hitler analogy in international affairs continues. Recently, as the Iraq-Kuwait crisis evolved, Hitler's Germany reemerged as the symbol of a nation gone wild. Some analysts described parallels between the Nazi Party and Saddam Hussein's emphasis on the Ba'th party as a carrier of pan-Arabism. Most importantly, top U.S. policymakers have not been adverse to invoking the Nazi analogy, with President Bush at one point suggesting that Hussein's use of Americans as shields against attack was even beneath the Nazi leader. "Hitler did not stake people out against potential military

1

targets," the President stated, "and he did...respect the legitimacy of the embassies."[4] All this has caused one columnist, an obviously exhausted veteran of the Containment years, to comment in exasperation:

> I don't know why people keep saying we don't have a good reason for going to war with Iraq. Of course we do; the same one we've had for every war we've fought in the past 45 years: We're going to war to stop Hitler. Ever since we missed our first chance to stop Hitler 50 years ago, we've been trying to make up for it; in Korea, in Cuba, in Vietnam, in Nicaragua, in El Salvador—in Grenada, for crying out loud—and now in Iraq.[5]

That observation notwithstanding, Hitler and his 12-year regime is a valuable startpoint in examining what have been called "crazy states," an increasingly important concept in the post-cold war era involving both the personal characteristics of national policymakers as well as the decision-making structure and processes of their states.[6] Historically, nation states like Gadhafi's Libya have emerged from time to time. But the majority remained isolated, local phenomena. Modern technology has changed this. The communications revolution now allows these states to achieve notoriety, if not status, in the international arena. Equally important, technology offers the potential for these countries to build up significant power to influence regional, if not global, events. Added to this is the breakdown of the superpower bipolar nexus which, while reducing East-West tensions, has also mitigated the pattern of client state stability. In such a multipolar, interdependent environment marked by the proliferation of conventional and nuclear weaponry, the capabilities and potential impact of a rogue or "crazy" state will be of increasing importance.

But what constitutes "craziness"? What variables can be applied for what will be, at least in part, culturally biased value judgments based on Western norms? In such a context, as will be demonstrated, pure rationality in the instrumental sense of being able to make means commensurate with ends is not enough. And yet by simultaneously holding up an ideal type of means-ends rational decisionmaking as the basis for comparison, and by opening up the "black box" of the unitary nation state in order to focus on the structure of government

2

and the personal characteristics of the decision makers, other criteria can emerge as a basis for evaluation.

The pure rationality model in Figure 1 is a "synoptic conception" of decision making, by which the policymaker places all available alternatives before him and measures, against his scale of preferred values, all the possible consequences of the various courses of action under consideration.[7]

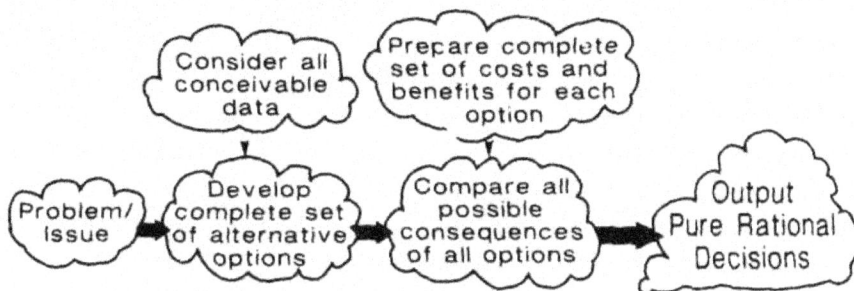

Figure 1. Pure Rational Decision Making.

The model is what Max Weber called an "ideal type," which, with few exceptions, is impossible to achieve since it presupposes omniscience and a capability for comprehensive analysis that time, cost and other factors simply do not permit. Nevertheless, as Weber pointed out, by using such types, "it is possible to understand the ways in which actual action is influenced by irrational factors of all sorts...that...account for the deviation from the line of conduct which would be expected on the hypothesis that the actions were purely rational."[8]

The so-called "black box" geopolitical strategic model superimposes the nation state on this pure rational typology. Key to this conceptualization is the idea that governments are rational, value maximizing actors in international affairs—black boxes with goals, whose behavior reflects purpose and intention. Scholars have pursued variations of the concept. Some have explored ideology, culture and national characteristics as explanations for the difference in state behavior.[9] Others have enhanced the usefulness of the "black box" concept by focusing on the elements of national power,

3

with variations determined by geostrategic theories.[10] The boxes, in other words, are not just black, but of varying colors depending un such elements as power, ideology and strategic position. But they remain boxes in the sense that the analysts do not have to know what goes on inside them, deducing from the actions of the boxes in the global arena the nature of their intentions.

Other scholars, however, have not been content with this model and its variants and have opened up the boxes in search of better explanations for the behavior of states, normally focusing on the personal characteristics of policymakers as well as the structure and concomitant decision-making processes of the government.[11] This study will take a similar approach with the black box of Nazi Germany. The inner decision-making workings of that 12-year regime will be compared with the pure rationality model as a basis for a first cut at inductive validation of general patterns and relationships from that era for use in evaluating the potential for emergence of "crazy" states and possible methods for dealing with them in an increasingly complex world.

CHAPTER 2

RATIONALITY AND THE MEANS-ENDS CONNECTION

The classic description of strategy as the calculated relationship of means to ends is in keeping with the ideal pure rationality model. Clausewitz, in fact, defined rationality in warfare as the commensurate relationship between violence as means and politics as ends in which war, governed by political calculation and reasoning, became not "a mere act of policy; but a true political instrument, a continuation of political activity by other means."[12] Basic to this approach is the assumption that means are not arbitrary in the sense of constituting subjective behavior that has no relation to any ends such as essentially random or strictly cathartic action. Instead, means are related to ends in a manner that can be justified in terms of positivistic instrumentality. Astrology, for instance, may be claimed subjectively to relate means to ends, but would be perceived objectively as unjustified and, therefore, irrational. Thus, irrationality can be said objectively to have governed the strategic decisions of Julius Caesar to the extent that those decisions were based on the patterns of chicken entrails.[13]

This abstract concept of instrumental rationality is acultural, but as one theorist has noted, "at a human level one man's god is another man's heresy, and manifestations of rationality, like those of religion, are a matter of geographical accidents and cultural heredity.C[14] In fact, cultural or, as in the case of Hitler, mental differences may prevent one nation from accepting or even perceiving certain options for another nation which in an objective instrumental sense may be fully rational. Clausewitz's dictum that war is a means to serve political ends, for instance, is open to varying interpretations. For the West, those political ends normally can only be served through military victory. As a consequence, a state acting in accordance with Western experience will never resort to war if it has little or no chance of winning militarily. Political goals, in short, cannot be achieved by defeat.

For many non-Western countries, on the other hand, war is considered a worthwhile means even if military success is not assured, so long as political and psychological goals can be achieved, to include such intangibles as the preservation of national honor and pride. The rational instrumentality of this "success through failure" approach is not easily grasped by Western states, which see it as a tendency in non-Western societies to assume much greater risks than those considered by Western standards to be rational or profitable. Thus, in the 1973 Yom Kippur war, Egyptian President Sadat was willing to risk military defeat to improve his political status, both of which came to pass. For the Israelis, the majority of whom perceive that there is no substitute for victory, there was little comprehension of a military offensive that *a priori* could not result in military victory. By projecting this different concept of instrumental rationality onto the Arab culture, the Israelis were unable to anticipate Egyptian behavior.[15]

In a similar manner, World War II began for the United States because, in part, of an inability to understand the Japanese readiness to accept risks that were unacceptable by American standards. The United States in 1941, one author noted, could not believe "that a power as small as Japan would make the first strike against a power as big as the United States.... Japanese sanity cannot be measured by our own standards" which "reckoned the risks to the Japanese as too large and therefore not likely to be taken."[16] And in the final months of that war, the divine wind sacrifice of the Kamikaze pilots was perceived by the U.S. military and public as a horrendously irrational tactic. For the hard-pressed Japanese elites, however, it seemed a rational means to sink enemy war ships.[17]

Cultural subjectivity, then, can hinder the objective evaluations of means and ends commensurability that essentially defines "rationality." For some theorists, this simply adds to the argument that such a definition is too narrow since it omits a discussion of values which, at the very least, influence the decision maker's appreciation of the situation and, as a consequence, the means-to-ends process associated with instrumental rationality.

> The choice of means, however these are conceived, is as much dictated by value-related ends as by strictly limited notions of capability. Rationality thus becomes normative in character and is related to justifiable action in terms of some ethical code or set of rules as much as to standards of effectiveness. If strategy is treated...as action directed to the fulfillment of political purposes, their instrumentality has to be related to the nature of these purposes. It is not a mechanical or teleological relationship between means and ends.[18]

Rationality, in other words, is not simply limited to a choice among means, but also includes the judgment of what values are worth pursuing. "The paranoid who waits till dark before turning on his persecutors may be a master strategist," Abraham Kaplan has pointed out in this regard; "he is surely not a paragon of rationality."[19] To admit otherwise, Kaplan adds, is to concede that Satan has a fine mind and is lacking only in heart. Goals must be examined beyond mere instrumentality, in order to demonstrate that Satan "is a fool from beginning to end."[20]

Most theorists, however, believe that the term "rational" can be used legitimately only to describe judgments or beliefs about matters of fact or logical relation, such as whether given means are adequate for the fulfillment of given ends. The term cannot be applied to ends themselves, since they are neither rational nor irrational. Instead, they represent values which are not the type of entity to which the conception of rationality is applicable since it involves the realm of moral judgment without an empirical referent. Thus, even in the pure rationality model, the formulation and prioritization of final values can only be determined by value judgments, not by rational processes, which creates, as Felix Oppenheim has pointed out, a different perspective on the Prince of Darkness.

> If Satan has a fine mind, he is no fool, but a rational actor, however diabolic his goals may appear to us. This is precisely why he is so dangerous, as are those wielders of absolute power who incarnate

him. Their scale of values may be abhorrent to us, but reason is of no avail to prove that they should act otherwise.[21]

The two approaches mean that rationality is a necessary but not sufficient factor upon which to base an examination of the concept of crazy states. On the one hand, the use of "morality" in the "rational" evaluation of goals, what Weber called *Zweckrationalität,* can, like the use of "realism," lead to doubtful judgments. In the early years of Hitler's rule, for instance, the anti-appeasers made a case for military intervention in Germany before the Nazi leader had consolidated his power. At that time, it was generally considered immoral to sacrifice lives for such an effort, although, as one of the leading anti-appeasers has pointed out, 30,000 casualties might have sufficed. In 1939, however, intervention was considered moral; but by that time, the action involved some 30,000,000 lives.[22]

On the other hand, to accept only the instrumental definition implicit in the pure rationality model can lead to moral realtivism which, as Ivan Karamazov observed, will inevitably lead to an "anything goes" position. Isaiah Berlin has noted in this regard that

> when we are told that it is foolish to judge Charlemagne, or Napoleon or Ghengis Kahn, or Hitler, or Stalin (or that such judgments are beyond the point, we can only answer that)...to accept this doctrine is to do violence to the basic notions of our morality, to misrepresent our sense of our past, and to ignore the most general concepts and categories of normal thought.[23]

The answer is to accept the objective, more limited definition of rationality while applying moral judgments at the same time as separate subjective, value-laden criteria. In this context, a state may behave rationally in an instrumental sense of effectively achieving its ends or goals which in themselves may be "crazy."[24]

CHAPTER 3

OPERATIONAL CODE AND THE COGNITIVE TRAIL

Decision-making structures within the governmental black box can range from single individuals to large bureaucracies, each invoking different types of processes for dealing with uncertainty and conflict among participants as well as for making and implementing choices. The size of these structures as well as the distribution of power and the roles of group members within the organization are among properties present in all decisions which insure the probability that certain decision processes are more likely to be used than others. Variations in these processes influence the foreign policy behavior selected by the decision maker(s). This in turn allows the strategic analyst to examine the impact of the personal characteristics of national leaders as well as the organizational processes on the rational decision-making model.

The duality is important, because there will inevitably be tendencies to focus on one to the detriment of the other. There has been, in fact, a great deal of controversy concerning the effect that a leader's personal characteristics can have on foreign policy. Some analysts contend that individual actors are limited in their effect on events by social forces—the so-called "great man" versus *Zeitgeist* debate. Others point to organizational constraints and the fact that political leaders are merely "agents" or representatives, reflecting the views, beliefs and ideologies of their constituencies and agencies. "Names and faces may change," one analyst has concluded in this regard, "interests and policies do not."[25] Most cases actually fall between the extremes, with theorists taking into account the total situation in which the decision makers act as well as their own traits. Political leadership in this context is "the interaction of personality, role, organization, task, values, and setting as expressed in the behavior of salient individuals."[26]

In the case of Nazi Germany, there is a broad historical school, the so-called "intentionalists," that views Hitler as the principal force in the Third Reich whose personality and ideology drove events, a perception summarized succinctly in one historian's conclusion that "the point cannot be stressed too strongly: Hitler was master in the Third Reich."[27] As opposed to those who see the absolute centrality of Hitler in the Third Reich, the "structuralist" or "functionalist" school focuses more on the structure of Nazi rule and the functional nature of policy decision making. As early as the 1940s, analysts had begun to challenge the concept of the rational "monolithic" Nazi state, pointing out that beyond the unitary facade of the Third Reich, the power structure seethed with personal and organizational rivalries, reminding a counsel at the Nuremberg trials of "the minor courts of the Italian Renaissance."[28] In more recent times, analysts have renewed the examination of how organizational processes and bureaucratic politics influenced decision making in Nazi Germany by focusing on the civil service, Party-State relations, the regional power bases of the Gauleiter, and policy implementation at local levels.[29]

An analysis of crazy states must also recognize this duality. Beginning with the political leader, his *Weltanschauung,* depending on the degree of his political control, will shape the strategies that his government will employ in its foreign policy. Because the personal characteristics that feed into this world view can structure the policymaker's interpretation of the environment, he will be likely to ensure, again depending on his control, that the government acts consistent with this image. A policymaker "acts upon his 'image' of the situation," one analyst has noted in this regard, "rather than upon 'objective' reality."[30] His *Weltanschauung,* in other words, forms the basis for the political leader's cognitive map that charts his course in overcoming the type of conditions which, as Alexander George has pointed out, normally accompany the rational decision-making process:

> (1) The political actor's information about situations with which he must deal is usually incomplete; (2) his knowledge of ends-means relationships is generally inadequate to predict reliably the

10

consequences of choosing one or another course of action; and (3) it is often difficult for him to formulate a single criterion by means of which to choose which alternative course of action is "best."[31]

Understanding this cognitive map—the so-called "Operational Code"—of a political leader can be an important tool for dealing with crazy states, since it sets the boundaries within which the leader will act. The code would include the actor's decision-making style as well as his philosophical and instrumental beliefs, which might be better labeled, in George's estimation, "approaches to political calculation."[32] These can range from orientation on opponents and notions about chance or risk to ideological goals and the ability and commitment to implement those goals—all important inputs needed for behavioral analysis of political decision making and leadership. The operational code is not a simple key to explanation and prediction, but as George has pointed out, "it can help...to 'bound' the alternative ways in which the subject may perceive different types of situations and approach the task of making a rational assessment of alternative courses of action."[33]

THE PERSONAL LINK

Any examination of decision making in a crazy state should begin with an investigation of the leader's beliefs about politics, which can be postulated as part of his operational code on the basis of generally accessible data. Hitler's thoughts on the "Jewish problem" and the acquisition of *Lebensraum* in the East, for instance, were two fundamental constants in his world view that were available in written form through *Mein Kampf* as early as the mid-1920s and were normally used in the Nazi leader's speeches both during the *Kampfzeit* and after he assumed power.[34] The emergence of such a belief system may be affected by developmental problems encountered in personality formulation, which should also be examined when possible. Walter Langer's wartime psychological study of Hitler, in this regard, was remarkably accurate in some respects, even to the conjecture of monorchidism (one testicle) on the part of the Nazi leader; and his analysis of Hitler's decision-making cognition pattern remains an insightful point of departure.

11

He does not think things out in a logical and consistent fashion, gathering all available information pertinent to the problem, mapping out alternative courses of action, and then weighing the evidence pro and con for each of them before reaching a decision. His mental processes operate in reverse. Instead of studying the problem, as an intellectual would do, he avoids it and occupies himself with other things until unconscious processes furnish him with a solution. Having the solution he then begins to look for facts that will prove that it is correct. In this procedure he is very clever, and by the time he presents it to his associates, it has the appearance of a rational judgment. Nevertheless, his thought processes proceed from the emotional to the factual instead of starting with the facts as an intellectual normally does. It is this characteristic of his thinking process that makes it difficult for ordinary people to understand Hitler or to predict his future actions. His orientation in this respect is that of an artist and not that of a statesman.[35]

Psychoanalytical examinations of crazy state leaders, however, should also be handled carefully. The concept of motivation, for example, is not only typically Western in its purposive behavior and degrees of freedom, but is extremely complex, often with any prioritization, when that can be even ascertained, being only fortuitous. In this regard, the German annexation of the Sudentenland, according to one former associate of the Nazi leader, was at least partially inspired at the 1937 Breslau festival, when participants from that province marched past the reviewing stand shouting demands for liberation from Czechoslovakia.[36] This points to two major problems in dealing with explanations of the phenomenon of crazy state leaders which depend for their validity on psychohistorical insights. To begin with, the conjectural element in any analysis of this kind will, of necessity, be extremely high, simply because patient diagnosis is at best secondhand. More importantly, however interesting an analysis of a national leader's psychopathology can be for understanding why he acts, it cannot explain or predict how the psychic tensions in that leader, even when diagnosed properly, are or will be translated into political action. How, in other words, is one to take Langer's conclusion that Hitler was "a

12

neurotic psychopath bordering on schizophrenia" and relate it to real world correctives in terms of crazy states.[37]

THE CULTURAL LINK

One way to move beyond the psychoanalytical approach is to recognize that the structure of expectations by policymakers as well as their perceptual interpretations, motivations and behavioral norms are directly affected by their society and culture. Certainly, decision makers, even those in crazy states, tend like everybody else to organize their cognition and perception of reality in terms of cultural meanings and values. "If triangles had a god," Montesquieu once remarked in this regard, "he would have three sides."[38] Common or similar values, in other words, are not necessary for understanding or attempting to predict the actions of crazy state leaders. But understanding the difference in values is absolutely essential.

Otherwise, the strategist of one nation will project his own values and sense of priorities on those of another state. "If my opponent is rational," the thought process goes in this circumstance, "he will do what any rational man would do in this situation. I am rational. Therefore he will do what I would do in his shoes. If I were in his shoes I would...." By this process, ethnocentrism sabotages one of the central thought processes in strategy—that of knowing the enemy. There is a need, in this regard, to realize as Andre Gide has pointed out, that "grey is the colour of truth."[39]

The distortion of threat perception, of course, can be deliberate on the part of a crazy state leader, further complicating the process. It is, in fact, not unusual for such leaders to use ethnocentrism to demonize or dehumanize outsiders, to create a foreign "Great Satan"—all in furtherance of Bertrand Russell's dictum that "few people can be happy unless they hate some other person, nation or creed."[40] Hitler played upon this concept throughout his career in order to intensify in-group/out-group feelings within German society and to make the population sensitive about German rights and interests. "Identifying enemies helps define who we are *not*,"

13

he wrote as early as 1925, "which is a necessary part of defining who we *are*."[41] And years later, when asked if the Jews should be destroyed, Hitler replied in the negative, adding that otherwise "we should have then to invent him. It is essential to have a tangible enemy, not merely an abstract one."[42]

In addition to threat perception, cultural relativism is particularly important in negotiating with crazy states since that process involves a psychological relationship in terms of bargaining and is therefore inevitably prone to the problems of ethnocentric perceptions. In the interwar years, for example, Allied diplomats were not prepared for the different styles, strategies and tactics of their counterparts in the totalitarian regimes. Western diplomacy had long put a premium on honesty and compromise. Hitler, on the other hand, viewed compromise as a sign of weakness, appreciated the instrumentality of the "big lie" over the small one, and believed that negotiating in good faith was, at the very least, a silly principle. In this context, appeasement could only be a sign of weakness for the Nazi leader. "Our enemies are little worms," he reassured his military leaders on August 22, 1939," "I saw them at Munich."[43]

Hitler's contempt for his adversaries was due in part to the ease with which he manipulated the perceptions of the Allies by masking his intentions to fit the beliefs of most Western European nations that any defeated, proud and powerful nation state would attempt to change an enforced peace treaty in order to regain a legitimate, but not dominating, position in world politics. What Hitler did not realize, however, was that the March 1939 annexation of rump Czechoslovakia convinced the Western Powers that what had appeared to be a policy of revisionist status quo in terms of the Versailles Treaty had really been from the start a policy of imperialism, of continental, if not worldwide dimensions. The result was that until the outbreak of war, the Nazi leader and the Western Powers were locked in a game of "chicken" by which either side could avoid collision by turning the steering wheels of their national vehicles headed at each other. The problem was that by that time, one side had metaphorically been conditioned to drive on the left hand side of the road, the other on the right. Under those conditions, attempts to engage in "rational" war avoiding strategic behaviors only helped precipitate confrontations.[44]

All this was illustrated on August 23, 1939 when the British Ambassador in Berlin personally delivered a letter from the British Prime Minister, Neville Chamberlain, to Hitler which began: "It has been alleged that if H.M. Government had made their position more clear in 1914 the great catastrophe would have been avoided."[45] The letter then went on to emphasize Britain's determination and resolve to honor the guarantee to Poland. Unfortunately, the Prime Minister also continued by pointing out that all issues between Germany and Poland could be settled by negotiations and suggested ways such a process could be initiated. For the Nazi leader, the British warning was vitiated by Chamberlain's familiar offer to continue his search for a peaceful solution. Added to this was his confidence that the actual conclusion of the German-Russian nonaggression pact would shake the resolution of the Western Allies. Acting on these misperceptions, on the evening of his interview with the British Ambassador, Hitler scheduled the German attack on Poland.

COGNITIVE DISSONANCE AND CONSISTENCY

This type of diplomatic denouement also reveals how far the cognitive trail of a policymaker can stray from the pure rational decision-making model. In that ideal type, all aspects of the problem are fully understood by the decision maker. In actuality, however, as several theorists have postulated, because most problems are too complex to allow a total or synoptic rationality, policymakers are forced to begin with existing problems and take incremental decision steps when issues arise, as shown in Quadrant 3 of Figure 2.[46] Thus, even in Nazi Germany, the first tentative steps in foreign affairs were nothing more than incremental "muddling through," with Hitler assuring visitors that there would "be no change in the policy...laid down in 1932."[47] These assurances were followed by Germany's continued membership in the European disarmament conference as well as the Nazi leader's so-called *Friedensrede* to the Reichstag, the conciliatory aspects of

15

```
                        CHANGE
U                Incremental    Large
N
D       ┌──────────────┬──────────────┐
E       │              │              │
R  High │      1       │      2       │
S       │              │              │
T       ├──────────────┼──────────────┤
A       │              │              │
N  Low  │      3       │      4       │
D       │              │              │
I       └──────────────┴──────────────┘
N
G
```

Figure 2.
Change and Understanding in Decision Making.

which "could scarcely have been equalled by Stresemann or Bruening."[48]

It is almost an historical cliche, of course, that German foreign policy in the interwar years moved increasingly into Quadrant 4 where decisions of ever greater import were made with incomplete information. For the Nazi dictator, however, always intolerant of ambiguity and moving with each foreign policy success in those years further into his own world of hubristic infallability, there were cognitive adjustments that allowed him in his own perception to move into Quadrant 2, "the realm of superhuman decision-makers."[49] The most common of such adjustments was Hitler's consistent tendency through the years to fit incoming information into his preexisting beliefs and hopes. In terms of his unfavorable opinion of Soviet capabilities, for example, when the two armies met in October 1939 at the German-Russian demarcation line in what had been Poland, Hitler was particularly interested in the reports of the bedraggled state of the Russian troops.[50]

16

One result of such developments, on the one hand, is cognitive dissonance in which decision makers like Hitler seek to increase their comfort level with strategies already implemented by minimizing any evidence that might lead to different conclusions. This tendency to make the enemy "fit" into a strategy that has been decided upon was demonstrated not only by Hitler, but by two generations of German leaders who convinced themselves that Great Britain would not enter into a continental war or that it would not be a major factor in such a war.

In Hitler's case, the process began with his conviction that the allied guarantee of Poland was not serious, a conviction bolstered by organizational and political deviations from the unitary rational actor model. Most noticeable, in this regard, was Joachim von Ribbentrop, the Nazi foreign minister, who provided a constant flow of information on a weakened, indecisive Britain to Hitler who, in turn, was happy to receive reinforcement of his own beliefs. If any member of the Wilhelmstrasse deviated from this position, Ribbentrop warned his subordinates at the time, he "would kill him myself in his office and take responsibility before the Fuehrer for it."[51] Based on such input, the British guarantee was perceived by Hitler as a bluff; and in the coming months, the Tripartite alliance with Italy and Japan and the Nazi-Soviet nonaggression pact were his counters to that bluff. How limited the Nazi leader's perception was of the danger in calling this bluff was demonstrated when he heard the news of the British ultimatum on September 3, 1939. "What now?" he demanded savagely of the hapless Ribbentrop.[52]

From Hitler's perception, the German-Polish war presented no threat to British and French vital interests and could have been treated as a limited conflict. From the standpoint of military technology as well as Poland's geographical position, the target for German aggression was far removed from both countries. Moreover, the German thrust into Poland eliminated that state's buffer role with the USSR, thus increasing the possibility of military confrontation between Germany and the Soviet Union. Britain and France, however, viewed the German invasion of Polish territory as part of a larger war in

17

which their national security was at stake. As a consequence, they entered into a conflict in which, as the astounded Hitler noted, the means adopted were both inadequate and incommensurate with the ends desired—a study in Clausewitzian instrumental irrationality. "(T)hink of the declaration of war in 1939!" he commented, still incredulous three years later. "They had no armaments at all—and yet they declared war!"[53]

Such manifestations of cognitive dissonance naturally increased in number and severity as the flow of events became more unacceptable. "The myth of our vulnerability, in the events of the war becoming prolonged, must be resolutely discarded," Hitler declared in 1941. "It's impermissible to believe that time is working against us."[54] Towards the end of the war, this had become the outright refusal to acknowledge the hopelessness of the situation. On March 15, 1945, for instance, Albert Speer prepared a memorandum for the Nazi leader that outlined the situation in stark terms. Hitler began to read the report, but when he came across the words, "The War is lost," he refused to read another line. And on another occasion during that period, General Guderian described Hitler's plaintive refusal of a request by Speer to meet with the Nazi leader alone.

> All he wants is to tell me again that the war is lost and that I should bring it to an end. Now you can understand why it is that I refuse to see anyone alone any more. Any man who asks to talk to me alone always does so because he has something unpleasant to say to me. I can't bear that.[55]

On the other hand, a case can be made for rational cognitive consistency on the part of the Nazi leader for much of his career, since his actions were based on what he perceived as constants in the environment and because within that construct, he did not violate generally agreed-upon rules for dealing with evidence.[56] How rational Hitler's cognitive pattern could be was illustrated by Operation Barbarossa. At the strategic level, the German underevaluation of Soviet strength not only made means and ends apparently more commensurate in an instrumental sense, but served to further the Nazi leader's logical conclusion that Russian military power

18

limitations militated against deferring an invasion. To begin with, there was the inevitability of war with the Soviet Union which had permeated his goal of Eastern *Lebensraum* since the beginning of the *Kampfzeit.* "Therefore," he concluded, "it's better to stave off the danger now, while we can still trust in our own strength."[57] Moreover, by 1941 the Nazi leader believed that Britain could not be conquered in the near future and that London's hope of Soviet support only served to prevent an Anglo-German settlement. At the same time, U.S. entry into the conflict seemed inevitable—a disastrous possibility if the Soviet Union remained intact, able to threaten Germany's rear or to cut off supplies it was providing the Third Reich. For Hitler, "the road to London passed through Moscow."[58]

This was particularly true since there was at least a year and a half breathing space before an Allied invasion of the Continent would be possible. The armored might of the Wehrmacht, sitting idly in the West since the conquest of France, could thus be used in this period to eliminate the Soviet Union and its rapidly growing military strength in order to avoid the traditional German nemesis of a two-front war. "Britain's hope lies in Russia and the United States," Hitler concluded. "If Russia drops out of the picture, America, too, is lost for Britain, because the elimination of Russia would greatly increase Japan's power in the Far East."[59]

Such rational grand strategic calculations notwithstanding, Hitler's ethnocentrically-based, ideologically-tinged underestimation of his Slavic opponent permeated down to the theater strategic and operational levels where it had disastrously irrational logistical results in terms of means-end commensurability. Using calculations of ammunition expenditure from the Western campaigns, for example, the Army planners swallowed any misgivings they might have had as they made new estimates conform with quantities German troops could carry. Even the original assessment of 5 months for conquering the Soviet Union was scaled down. By the time Barbarossa was launched, there was no buffer in the planning for flexible solutions to unexpected problems. "Rather than culling down their goals to suit their limited means," Martin van

Creveld has pointed out concerning the German planners, "they persuaded themselves that their original calculations were overcautious."[60]

CHAPTER 4

STYLE

The style of policymakers encompasses personal methods of making decisions based on operational codes and might include preferences for compromising and optimizing as well as for such components as confidence and openness to new information. Or it might include, at an interpersonal level, how a leader views his environment in dealing characteristically with other policymakers, which in turn might entail an examination of his use of threats and praise to persuade, his sense of political timing or his sensitivity to other leaders. Above all, in terms of crazy state analysis, the examination of a leader's style should focus on deviations from what is regarded as normal behavior in international actions—that is, the propensity and preference (conscious or unconscious) for stylistic innovations which are not constrained by accepted patterns such as the hijacking of aircraft and the seizure of diplomats as hostages.[61]

In Hitler's case, the first indications of such deviations were in domestic politics, beginning with the systematic use of terror after the February 1933 Emergency Decrees and the "Blood Purge" of Röhm and the SA in June 1934. For the Nazi leader, normal rules and conventions must be swept away when, at "critical periods in history all the tinsel falls away and the great rhythm of life alone rules the hour."[62] At such a point, he had no choice. "I must do things that cannot be measured with the yardstick of bourgeois squeamishness."[63]

> If these gentlemen, with their outworn ideas, imagine that they can go on pursuing policy like the honest merchant with his business, in accordance with precedent and convention, let them go on. But I am concerned with power politics—that is to say, I make use of all means that seem to me to be of service, without the slightest concern for the proprieties or for codes of honor.... I certainly have an advantage...in my freedom from pedantic and

sentimental inhibitions. Am I to be so generous as to throw away this advantage, simply because my opponents have not progressed so far? If anyone is prepared to be deceived, he must not be surprised that he is.... It is characteristic of the narrowness of these outlived classes that they should be indignant with me, indignant at our contempt for past customs and assumptions in political life. I recognize no moral law in politics. Politics is a game, in which every sort of trick is permissible, and in which the rules are constantly being changed by the players to suit themselves.[64]

PRAGMATISM, TECHNIQUE AND HUBRIS

These statements notwithstanding, there was a pragmatic side to Hitler which can often mark the leaders of crazy states with their authoritarian ability to subordinate ideology to national interests. Thus, there was the August 1939 Nazi-Soviet nonaggression pact in which Hitler's diplomatic surprise prepared the way for a military surprise. In *Mein Kampf*, he had pointed out the "tactical considerations" for such an alliance. And a decade later, he returned to the theme in his discussions of the need to conquer the great spaces of the Soviet Union. "That does not mean that I will refuse to walk part of the road together with the Russians, if that will help us," he concluded. "But it will be only in order to return the more swiftly to our true aims."[65]

Pragmatism also includes an ability to learn from failure. The classic case with Hitler was his abortive 1923 putsch in Munich. From that failure, the Nazi leader not only learned that he could not prepare for battle with the power of the German state on a purely Bavarian plane, but that *Konflikt* itself was not a suitable means to his end. "It will take longer, to be sure," he declared, "to outvote our opponents than to outshoot them, but in the end their own Constitution will give us success."[66]

After he achieved that success, Hitler continued to employ the dual approach as a rational and conscious means to overcome all opposition. On the domestic front there was the process of *Gleichschaltung*, or coordination, in which every breach of the law or the Constitution was camouflaged and accompanied by vociferous claims to respect legality. It was, in fact, a classic case of a rational, totalitarian capture of

22

democratic machinery with the assistance of, not in opposition to, the state. The key to the process was the linkage of legal and revolutionary actions which produced an overarching screen of legality, dubious in individual instances and yet convincing enough as a whole to keep the essential illegal construct of the regime hidden. As a consequence, certain areas of public life like civil law were initially untouched leaving, in this example, reassuring preserves which made it difficult to assess the regime's legality and, as a consequence, whether it should be supported or not. Many people, in this regard, hoped to domesticate the revolutionary side of the revolution—an illusion that was fostered by a nationalistic smoke screen that ultimately persuaded the civil service, the Army, the political parties, the trade unions and the legal profession to support totalitarian goals.[67]

In a similar manner in foreign affairs, force was always accompanied by expressions of scruples and protestations of peaceful intent. From 1933 to 1936, for example, a time of relative weakness for Germany in the international arena, Hitler's diplomacy of *fait accomplis* increased his adopted country's strength while carefully and rationally avoiding retaliation. In order to accomplish this, he inaugurated a pattern of diplomacy completely in keeping with his parvenu and revolutionary background and his disrespect for bourgeois values, but so alien to diplomatic norms that it shrouded, at least temporarily, the Nazi leader's intentions.

Each *fait accompli* would start and end with firm declarations of Germany's desire for peace and for friendly collaboration followed by new proposals for disarmament and nonaggression treaties. And because sanctions were still a possibility in the early years, Hitler issued a solemn promise after each diplomatic surprise that there would be no more such actions and that he would personally guarantee each of Germany's treaty obligations, particularly the one that was next on his repudiation list. In these promises, however, Hitler added the important condition that he would stand behind Germany's treaty obligations and remain peaceful only so long as the other international players followed suit. To this condition, the Nazi leader then invariably set other conditions that he knew were unacceptable to the nations involved, thus leaving each post-*fait accompli* speech with the normally unnoticed justification for the next *fait accompli*.[68]

For the leader of a crazy state, such deviations from diplomatic norms may be the rule. Like Hitler, surprise and shock tactics will have been most likely, in some form, the tools in the leader's rise to power and will thus continue to play a role in foreign policy after assumption of power. "Our present struggle is merely a continuation on the international level," Hitler declared in this regard, "of the struggle we waged on the national level."[69] Moreover, the very centrality of such a leader's power will ensure a large measure of control and, thus, diplomatic surprise. In the March 7, 1936 Rhineland crisis, for example, Hitler issued all orders on short notice. As a consequence, the operations divisions of the Wehrmacht services had less than a day to plan and then issue orders to their relevant departments. At the most, the Nazi leader only confided in nine people in late February and early March as the decision process was underway. Most of his Cabinet did not learn about the operation until late on the night of March 6; and most of the participating troops did not realize the nature of their true objective until they crossed into the demilitarized zone.[70]

That same crisis also illustrated how the ethics of "old school" diplomacy played a major role in the general inability to anticipate the actions of the Nazi leader. Professional diplomats simply found it difficult to accept the fact of Hitler's revolutionary diplomacy in which lies and deceit were basic to an approach that accepted no conventional obligations and that constantly used diplomatic instruments and language for deception. "I shall shrink from nothing," the Nazi leader confided in this regard. "No so-called international law, no agreements will prevent me from making use of any advantage that offers."[71] As a consequence, in the weeks preceding the Rhineland coup, the German Foreign Ministry issued no less than nine assurances that Germany had no intention of repudiating the Locarno Pact. Moreover, there was no rise in diplomatic tensions of the type that normally precede the

24

breaking of a diplomatic pact, no formal ultimatums or demands, and, in fact, Hitler even did his best to maintain normal relations with France during the period.[72]

Added to this was Hitler's unique sense of timing. His move into the Rhineland was originally planned for the spring of 1937, but the international conditions in the winter of 1936 caused him to change his mind. Like his March surprise of the previous year, the Rhineland move took place on a weekend when Western diplomats were normally absent from their capitols, thus providing initial insurance against prompt diplomatic reaction. The move also occurred at a time when relations between Britain and Italy, two of the Locarno guarantors, were at a particularly low ebb over Ethiopia. Moreover, it was a period when French public opinion was firmly opposed to any military action beyond the borders of France. And with the 7th of March only a few days prior to the French general elections (not to mention the Easter holiday), French leaders were not ready to take decisive action in anticipation or reaction to the German move.[73]

After 1936, this "diplomacy by challenge" soon reached its natural limits, a development noted by an official of the Wilhelmstrasse who called it as early as 1937 a policy of "accelerating the Last Judgment."[74] Others at home and abroad were not so prescient. By that time, the vitriolic style of discourse that marked the diplomacy of Nazi Germany and other totalitarian regimes had become so normal that messages which in former years would have meant hostilities, if not war, were by 1941 accepted as demonstrating mild protest. As a consequence, when the Japanese foreign minister made a blunt and hostile statement in May 1941 to the American ambassador, "in Washington no one made much ado about his words. Hitler had hardened statesmen to the whole vocabulary of abuse."[75]

Long before 1941, however, Hitler's diplomatic coups had come to an end in accordance with the adage that nothing fails like success. Paradoxically in this regard, hubris is based on an excessive belief in reason—a penalty, in other words, for success due to a reliance on successful techniques that eventually fall to a new challenge. Thus, as we have seen,

25

when it came to the Polish issue in 1939, Hitler did not realize in his preoccupation with his successful strategy that his success had undermined the conditions that made it possible. Because Britain and France had not fought before when Germany was weaker, he believed in the summer of that year that they would not fight for Poland. What the Nazi leader failed to realize was that his opponents who had succumbed at Munich were by that time ready to behave differently for many reasons, not the least of which was that the uninterrupted chain of Hitler's triumphs in foreign affairs had convinced them that his ambitions were unlimited.[76]

The nemesis of having wishes completely fulfilled applies as much to politics as to personal life, as Hitler repeatedly demonstrated. For the Nazi leader, reason alone did not suffice to guard against its own excesses. "That is the miracle of our age," he stated, "that you have found me, that you have found me among so many millions. And that I have found you, that is Germany's good fortune." In the end, dazzled by his successes and corrupted by arrogance and impatience fused in a hubristic infallibility, Hitler returned to the extra-legal solution discarded so many years before as a means to his ends: a putsch on a monstrous scale.[77]

PERSONAL STYLES AND THE STRUCTURE OF DECISION MAKING

To the more general style of interacting in the international arena, the analysts of crazy states should add the personal decision-making styles of the leaders, which can provide insights not only into deviations from the pure rationality model, but into the very nature of the governments themselves. The popular image of Hitler, for example, as an energetic and decisive policymaker does not stand up to scrutiny. In fact, as Karl Dietrich Bracher has pointed out, all the great decisions in the Nazi leader's life were actually acts of avoidance, whether it was leaving school and moving to Vienna, entering politics almost as a last resort, or launching World War II.[78] In this context, Hitler was a study in irresoluteness, normally allowing chance to govern developments and making decisions only when circumstances or opponents provided him no other

26

choice. What he termed *Schicksal* (destiny) or *Vorsehung* (province), in this regard, was nothing more than rationalization of his unwillingness to make decisions.

The discipline involved in regular work had always been anathema to the Nazi leader who believed that "a single idea of genius is worth more than a whole lifetime of conscientious office work."[79] As a consequence, after becoming Chancellor, Hitler reverted to form, returning to the idle bohemian style of the Vienna cafes and rejecting any administrative duties that smacked of what he had contemptuously termed, as an 18-year-old, *Brotberuf*, a "bread and butter" trade. One result was increasingly longer absences from Berlin in order to avoid official duties. Soon he settled in as Chancellor to a daily pattern of leaden inactivity, only occasionally breaking into manic restlessness, creating the lasting impressions of breathless effort from these spurts of abrupt frantic activity. When war came, he could only look longingly back on these peacetime work habits. "When peace has returned," he remarked in 1942, "I'll begin by spending three months without doing anything."[80] The work forced upon Hitler as war lord took a physical and mental toll, the latter as Joachim Fest has pointed out, because the work schedule "did violence to his nature and was in deliberate opposition to his inveterate yearning for passivity and indolence."[81]

These nonbureaucratic habits and idiosyncratic style of governing also contributed to the chaotic nature of the Third Reich. For example, Hitler was adverse to putting anything down on paper, and his lengthy absences from the capitol meant that he was increasingly unaccessible to even his top ministers. Added to this was his continued impatience with the complex details of intricate problems, and his tendency to seize compulsively upon stray pieces of information or ill-considered analysis from his paladins and court favorites in his inner circle. "Ministerial skill," it has been pointed out in this regard, "consisted in making the most of a favourable hour or minute when Hitler made a decision, thus often taking the form thrown out casually, which then went its way as an 'Order of the Führer.'"[82]

27

All this, of course, was a far cry from the pure rationality model for decision making, with the effective transfer to state administration of the Nazi Party's (NSDAP) basic social Darwinistic principle of letting things develop until the strongest had won. As a consequence, by the mid-1930s, influence in key state decisions had passed to the rotating cast of cronies in Hitler's inner circle, with governmental ministries effectively cut off from the process. In this inner circle, Martin Borman became the "Brown Eminence" in the declining years of the regime, a man of "darkness and concealment," as Richelieu called Père Joseph, the sinister prototype of anonymous power-seekers, a functionary who derived his power solely from his office. Borman filled all the key posts in the party with men who owed these powers to him personally, not because of past service or qualifications. Within a short time, his intimate knowledge of Hitler's personal peculiarities and weaknesses gave him decided advantages over his rivals, ensuring that he was keeper of the mystic gate right up to the moment of Hitler's suicide.[83]

To some degree, the institutional chaos in the Third Reich was a result of Hitler's calculated policy of "divide and rule." This does not mean, however, that there was a consistent and systematic strategy on his part in terms of that policy.[84] In some cases, for example, the Nazi leader promoted the establishment of huge power bases, the most notable being the tremendous accretion of political strength which Himmler and Goring enjoyed with Hitler's active support. In addition, as we have seen, there was the case of Martin Borman, who accumulated unprecedented power during the war without any anxiety being evidenced by the Führer. Finally, there was the intense danger posed by Ernst Röhm and the SA in the early phase of the dictatorship, which Hitler eliminated only after intense pressure from the Army as well as Himmler and Goring.

The domestic chaos was also due, in part, to Hitler's charismatic form of leadership which, in essence, rejected the institutional and bureaucratic norms required for the "rational" governing of a modern state in favor of dependence on personal loyalty to the Führer as the basis of authority. This transference of the NSDAP ethos from the *Kampfzeit* to a

28

modern government also led to the Nazi leader's almost pathological hypersensitivity to any attempts to impose the slightest institutional or legal restrictions upon his authority, which in the *Führerstaadt* had to be completely untrammelled and, in theory, absolute. "Constitutional law in the Third Reich," the head of the Nazi Lawyers Association stated in 1938, "is the legal formulation of the historic will of the Führer, but the historic will of the Führer is not the fulfillment of legal preconditions for his activity."[85] As a consequence, Hitler grew increasingly distrustful of any form of institutional loyalty and authority, whether it was demonstrated by army officers and civil servants or by lawyers, judges and church leaders.[86]

The corollary to this distrust of institutional links was Hitler's reemphasis on the personal loyalty, which had marked the basis of his charismatic authority from early *Kampfzeit* days, until it was elevated to a dominant governmental principle. As long as that loyalty remained intact, the Nazi leader, as we have seen, had no problem with power bases emerging from his own chosen knights in the inner circle based on his Führer authority. But when it failed, there was the corresponding distress as he demonstrated by his behavior in the *Tiefbunker* at the end when notified of the treachery by Himmler, his "loyal Heinrich."[87]

Nevertheless, the loyalty principle remained the bond between all followers and the person of the leader, bringing an almost neo-feudal aspect to the Reich. In fact, however, as Ian Kershaw has pointed out,

> the bonds of personal loyalty—a pure element of 'charismatic' rule—did not replace but were rather superimposed upon complex bureaucratic structures. The result was not complete destruction as much as parasitic corrosion. The avoidance of institutional restraints and the free rein given to the power ambitions of loyal paladins offered clear potential for the unfolding of dynamic, but unchannelled, energies—energies, moreover, which were inevitably destructive of rational government order.[88]

CHAPTER 5

RISK

Risk propensity on the part of decision makers is an important dimension in the analysis of crazy states. There are major problems in evaluation, however, many already encountered in the cognitive deviations from the pure rationality model. To begin with, the concept is directly related to instrumental rationality, a connection expressly made in John Collin's definition of risk as the "danger of disadvantage, defeat, or destruction that results from a gap between ends and means."[89] And yet crazy state leaders may not perceive the gap as dangerous or even that it exists. In terms of the former, as we have seen, in some countries where there are concepts of martyrdom or nobility in failure, the element of risk may hardly apply in some instances. When that is translated to foreign policy moves on the part of a particular country, U.S. policymakers, who generally prefer low risk alternatives in strategic options, often label such moves as "reckless behavior, brinksmanship and adventurism."[90]

More common are the cases where some states that use force to alter the status quo may differ from others less in the willingness to take perceived risks, than in the perception of low risks where others perceive high ones. In many of Hitler's "Saturday surprises" in the 1930s, for instance, the Nazi leader may have been "reckless," not because he willingly tolerated a high probability of conflict, but because he was certain that the other side would back down. When the German military opposed such policies as the Rhineland coup and the *Anschluss* on the basis that they were too dangerous, Hitler did not argue that the risks were worth the prizes, but that, instead, the risks were negligible—in other words, in terms of Figure 3, the MAXIMIN approach of Quadrant 2, not that of MAXIMAX in Quadrant 1.[91]

31

RISK

		HIGH (MAX)	LOW (MIN)
G A I N	HIGH (MAX)	1 MAXIMAX	2 MAXIMIN
	LOW (MIN)	3 MINIMAX	4 MINIMIN

Figure 3. Strategic Risk and Gain.

For example, in the Rhineland episode of March 7, 1936, the correlation of forces was quantifiably against Germany, as Hitler was well aware. "We had no army worth mentioning," he reflected later; "at that time it would not even have had the fighting strength to maintain itself against the Poles."[92] But, unlike military advisors focused firmly on French capabilities, the Nazi leader examined all the instruments of power, particularly national will, and concluded that France had no intention of responding militarily, thus decreasing in his mind a risk already mitigated, as we have seen, by the timing of the reoccupation.[93] The difference between Hitler's focus on intentions and the German military's necessary attention to capabilities only increased tensions as the crisis heightened. On March 9, the Wehrmacht commander received warning of impending French military countermoves and asked to withdraw troops from major cities in the Rhineland. But the Nazi leader, still taking an essentially MAXIMIN (Quadrant 2) approach, discounted the possibility of French intervention.[94]

The Rhineland coup also illustrated how Hitler deliberately fostered a MAXIMAX (Quadrant 1) picture of himself in international relations throughout the 1930s, accomplishing the extremely difficult job of projecting an image of a leader willing to pay a high cost to prevail in a specific dispute, but not willing to contest higher issues. The trick, as the Nazi leader realized, was to convince others of his willingness to go to war over a relatively minor issue by tying his stand to principles with more general applicability—in his case, those provided by the

Versailles Treaty. By couching his demands in terms of the generally perceived legitimate right to reverse that treaty rather than the general righting of previous wrongs, Hitler convinced others that the vehemence of these demands was not a harbinger of unlimited aggressiveness.[95]

The allied guarantee of Poland and subsequent declaration of war over the issue illustrate two important aspects in terms of risk propensity and crazy states. First the lack of rationally instrumental means on the part of the allies, as we have seen, caused Hitler to discount the guarantee in MINIMAX (Quadrant 3) if not MAXIMAX (Quadrant 1) terms. *"The men of Munich will not take the risk,"* he told his commanders at Obersalzberg on August 14, 1939.[96] Second, Hitler's actions illustrate that there is always the possibility that a crazy state may not perceive the extent to which its actions will change the status quo. A.J.P. Taylor has argued in this regard that the Nazi leader was quite possibly attempting to achieve "international equality" for Germany without comprehending that "the inevitable consequence of fulfilling this wish was that Germany would become the dominant state in Europe."[97] For the nations that had to deal with the Nazi state in close proximity, however, as Robert Jervis has pointed out, "this distinction was important only if they could alert Germany to the consequences of her actions and Germany would then modify her policies. If this was not possible, it mattered little whether Germany was attempting to dominate out of inadvertence or design."[98]

Risk propensity for a leader like Hitler is also dependent on the flow of accurate information. German preparations for Barbarossa, for instance, were marked by atrocious intelligence, resulting in gross underestimations of Soviet power by the German military and Hitler, who less than a year later remarked that "if someone had told me that the Russians had ten thousand tanks, I'd have answered: "You're completely mad!'"[99] Even so, the Nazi leader hovered nervously between the upper quadrants of the gain-risk matrix. "I never closed an eye during the night of...the 21st to 22nd of June 1941," he reported later, also remarking that if he had known how large the Soviet forces were, he never would have initiated the operation.[100] Nevertheless, it should not be

33

forgotten that Barbarossa was a very near thing—a point that suggests as Richard Betts has indicated, "how thin the line may be between foolhardiness and masterstroke and how deceptive hindsight can be about actual risks before the fact."[101]

The interplay of intelligence and risk is also a reminder of how important the concepts of preemptive attack and preventive war are in terms of the rational gain-risk matrix. A preemptive attack is concerned with immediate threats and is designed to take the initiative once strategic warning of enemy attack preparations are received. Even for an actor as blatantly aggressive as Hitler, the defensive motivation inherent in such attacks cannot be discounted. The German attack on Norway, for example, was a form of preemption, since the Nazi leader was aware that Britain was about to launch a strike into that country. And a few weeks later, Hitler's impatience to attack into the Lowlands can be explained, in part, by his fear that the Western allies might move first.[102]

Preventive war, on the other hand, is conducted in anticipation of future vulnerability on the part of the aggressor and is designed to take on an adversary before that adversary's capabilities can be improved. With Hitler and Barbarossa, for example, there is abundant evidence that preventive war in terms of his anxieties about growing German vulnerability reinforced his inclination to take risks for his long-held aggressive goals in the East. "What confirmed me in my decision to attack without delay," he recalled in 1942, "was the information...that a single Russian factory was providing by itself more tanks than all our factories together."[103] Time, in this construct, could only work against Germany. "If Stalin had been given another ten or fifteen years, Russia would have become the mightiest State in the world...."[104]

Added to this was the Nazi leader's perception that Stalin was increasingly intolerant of German conquests in the West and his own intolerance concerning Soviet annexations in the Balkans and Eastern Europe. In November 1940, Hitler offered Molotov, the Soviet foreign minister, a chance for the USSR to share in the booty and expand southward toward the Persian Gulf and India as the British Empire retreated. Molotov

34

replied by indicating Soviet intentions to occupy all of Finland; and later, as he and Ribbentrop sat out a British bombing raid in a Berlin shelter, he revealed to his German counterpart that the Soviets were interested in the Western approaches to the Baltic. "He demanded that we give him military bases on Danish soil on the outlets to the North Sea," Hitler still recalled with incredulity in the last week of his life. "He had already staked a claim to them. He demanded Constantinople, Romania, Bulgaria, and Finland—and we were supposed to be the victors."[105]

In addition, during this period, there was Hitler's continued lack of accurate intelligence on the Soviets that fed, as we have seen, into his rational strategic calculation that the road to London led through Moscow. Risk thus became acceptable for Barbarossa when the cost of not attacking the Soviet Union became unacceptable—a rational enough calculus, the "irrationality" of which in Stalin's perception ensured German military surprise. As a consequence of all this, the preventive war rationalization was strongly present the following month in Hitler's directive which stipulated that necessary measures were to be carried out "as a precaution against the possibility of the Russians adopting an attitude towards us rather than what it had been up to now."[106] For Stalin, this aspect of the Nazi leader's motivation was lost in his preoccupation with the danger of a German preemptive attack—a danger that, in the Soviet leader's estimation, would be increased by any improvements in Soviet readiness, since such actions would provoke rather than deter. As a result, Stalin never considered countermobilization, one of the worst ways to deter preemption, but the best way to deter preventive war.[107]

The "irrationality" of Barbarossa in the Soviet leader's perception reemphasizes the fact that crazy state leaders may logically try to close the instrumental risk gap between means and ends by various techniques. Hitler, in this regard, was certainly aware that military surprise was one such way. The invasion of the Lowlands in the spring of 1940, for instance, demonstrated the Nazi leader's appreciation of the paradox that the greater the risk, the greater the surprise, producing as a result less risk—a move by means of theater operational technique from MAXIMAX (Quadrant 1) to MAXIMIN (Quadrant 2). On the other hand. when the means-end gap was extremely wide and could not be closed in an operation like the invasion of England, Hitler backed off. Thus there is the picture of the Nazi leader sitting through interminable conferences on Sea Lion in the summer of 1940, sifting logically through Service squabbles and fluctuating estimates of the correlation of forces. Whether he was operating at that time from the MINIMAX (Quadrant 3) position because, as Admiral Raeder concluded, "in Hitler's opinion the war was already won," or the MAXIMAX position (Quadrant 1), Hitler made the logical decision for postponement based on his staff's final estimate on September 10, 1940, the day before he was to give the executive order:

> The weather conditions which for the time of year are completely abnormal and unstable, greatly impair transport movements and mine-sweeping activities for 'Sea Lion.' It is of decisive importance for the judgment of the situation, that no claim can be made to the destruction of the enemy air force over Southern England and the Channel area.... The English bombers...and the minelaying forces of the British Air Force, as the experiences of the last few days show, are still at full operational strength, and it must be confirmed, that the activity of the British forces has undoubtedly been successful.... The operational state,which the Naval War Staff...gave as the most important prerequisite for the operation, has so far not been achieved, i.e. clear air superiority in the Channel area and the extinction of all possibilities of enemy Air Force action in the assembly areas of the Naval Force, auxiliary vessels, and transports.[108]

As the war dragged on, however, the risks associated with the means-end gap at the grand strategic and theater strategic levels grew too great for the Nazi leader to cope with. Consequently, he "tacticalized" strategy, increasingly confining himself to the operational and tactical levels of war where he could still find some measure of means-ends commensurability. Thus, in contrast to Churchill's use of the Chiefs of Staff system, Hitler created the OKW to deal with grand strategic matters while he played operational commander of the army in the East without having to face the increasingly grim strategic problems. "The other day I called off an attack that was to procure us a territorial gain of four kilometres," Hitler recounted with obvious relish midway through the war, "because the practical benefit of the operation didn't seem to me to be worth the price it would have cost."[109] How far this descent to rationality had gone by the final year of the war was described in one instance by General Blumentritt:

> The plan came to us...in the most minute detail. It set out the specific divisions that were to be used.... The sector in which the attack was to take place was specifically identified and the very roads and villages through which the forces were to advance were all included. All this planning had been done in Berlin from large-scale maps and the advice of the generals...was not asked for, nor was it encouraged.[110]

CHAPTER 6

THE EXTRARATIONAL FACTOR

All policymakers rely on extrarational means to some extent because of limited resources, uncertain conditions and lack of knowledge—the normal barriers to pure rational decision making. There appears to be no way to make a valid normative model from the extrarational process, primarily because there is no way to compare the quality of a policy derived by means of subconscious processes such as intuition and judgment or thorough the interplay of charisma and ideology. What is certain, however, is that the extrarational factor is an important dimension of analysis in dealing with leaders of crazy states that can also account partly for the difficulty in predicting the foreign policy decisions of those actors. Moreover, the efficacy of extrarational decision making should not be discounted when examining these leaders. For example, in the two person, non-zero-sum, noncooperative version of the "Prisoner's Dilemma" shown in Figure 4, it can be demonstrated that extrarational decision making is better than that of pure rationality.[111]

In this version, two robbers are arrested in a stolen car and jailed separately. The police have evidence that they stole the car, but not that they committed the robbery. If both remain silent, each will be convicted only of the car robbery and each will receive a sentence of 3 years in prison. The prosecutor approaches the prisoners separately, promising each one that if he also confesses to the robbery and is the only one to make this full confession by a given time, he will be acquitted, while the other prisoner will be convicted on both counts and receive a 15-year sentence. When each prisoner than asks what happens if both of them confess, the prosecutor replies that the two prisoners will be convicted on both counts, but will receive relatively lighter sentences of 10 years because of their confessions.

	Prisoner B	
	No Confession	Confession
No Confession	A - 3 Years B - 3 Years	A - 15 Years B - 0 Years
Confession	A - 0 Years B - 15 Years	A - 10 Years B - 10 Years

(Row labels: Prisoner A)

Figure 4. Prisoner's Dilemma.

If both prisoners use pure rationality to make their decisions, their considerations would follow this pattern: "If the other guy confesses (or keeps quiet), should I confess or keep quiet? I should confess, never mind what he does, because if he keeps quiet, zero years in prison is better than 3 years; and if he confesses, 10 years in prison is better than 15." As a consequence of this rational decision making, both prisoners talk and spend 10 years in prison contemplating the limitations of pure rationality.

THE GREAT SIMPLIFIER

There is a normal bias on the part of policymakers towards "intuition" rather than "information" and towards "guess" rather than "estimate." Ideally, the optimum solution is to strengthen the rational components as much as possible in order to achieve some form of "informed intuition" or "guesstimate." The degree to which policymakers disregard such components can have a direct effect on the degree of "craziness" in their states, particularly if their decisions are bound up in a self-image of what Thomas Carlyle classified as the intuitive heroic figure who:

> brings events to pass that emanate directly from a rare ability to see through appearance and the plethora of detail, to discount the false and trivial, and to highlight the great and the tragic. His source of wisdom does not come from empirical knowledge. He has an intuitive sense of reality that allows him to feel and grasp new and unusual possibilities that otherwise are hidden to the senses. He cannot objectively prove what he so strongly feels. But when the event which was shaped by the force of the hero comes to pass, his people recognize the need if not the logical fitness of his deed.[112]

Hitler clearly saw himself in this mold—as one who could pierce the intricate complexities of the modern world. "I have the gift," he remarked in 1932, "of reducing all problems to their simplest foundations."[113] In that process, he was guided by a "divine Providence" that protected him throughout his career. *Mein Kampf* is studded with such references. It was fate that caused him to be born so close to the German frontier; that sent him to Vienna to suffer with the masses; that spared him in World War I, etc.—all for a larger purpose. "Divine Providence," he concluded, "has willed it that I carry through the fulfillment of the German task."[114]

Allied to this was the inner intuitive voice provided in "the commands that Providence has laid upon me," which governed his decisions. "No matter what you attempt," Hitler stated in this regard,

> if an idea is not yet mature, you will not be able to realize it. I know that as an artist, and I know it as a statesman. Then there is only one thing to do: have patience, wait, try again, wait again. In the subconscious, the work goes on. It matures, sometimes it dies. Unless I have the inner, incorruptible conviction, *this is the solution*, I do nothing. Not even if the whole party tries to drive me to action. I will not act; I will wait, no matter what happens. But if the voice speaks, then I know the time has come to act.[115]

The intuitive process reinforced a natural tendency of the Nazi leader to procrastinate, evident in his refusal to make up his mind in 1932 to stand as a presidential candidate and in his initial attempt to defer action against Raahm in 1934. Such inaction drove his advisors to distraction. But Hitler was adamant. "Trust your instincts, your feelings, or whatever you like to call them," he admonished. "Never trust your knowledge."[116] And when pressed for an explanation of his intuitive process, the Nazi leader fell back on his earlier vocation. "Do you know how an artist creates? In the same way the statesman must allow...his own thoughts to mature...."[117]

On the other hand, Hitler's "inner voice" at the subconscious level certainly accounted, in part, for his ability to penetrate difficult problems and to time his moves. Thus, there was his correct insistence against all advice throughout the latter part of 1932 on holding out for the Chancellorship. And, as we have seen, there was his perceptive, intuitive analysis of the situation during the Rhineland crisis. "I follow my course," he stated at that time, "with the precision and security of a sleepwalker."[118] This was the essence of Carlyle's hero figure who with his cry of "Act or you may never" transcends the power of reason and sense experience with his intuitive awareness. Apparent hesitations are swept away with one instantaneous, decisive blow. "The spirit of decision," Hitler observed, "consists simply in not hesitating when an inner conviction commands you to act...."[119]

IDEOLOGY AND CHARISMA

In *The Brothers Karamazov*, Dostoyevsky pointed out that the Church showed no tendency to become a "state," but that the state did all it could to become a church. Faith in this context is a major point of examination when analyzing a crazy state, particularly if it relegates reason to a subordinate role as was the case with medieval Christianity and with Hitlerism. The result can be state fanaticism which not only ignores values incompatible with those fanatically pursued, but, by ignoring the gravity of potential problems and obstacles, also removes national decision making from anything approaching

42

the instrumental rational process. In such cases, an increasingly interdependent world may no longer be willing to tolerate the principle *cuius regio; eius religio.*[120]

In the case of the Third Reich, there was nothing original in Hitler's ideology—a basic admixture of Social Darwinian thought and *Völkisch* themes tied in with Pan-Germanism, all espousing anti-Semitism and German superiority linked through concepts of "race" and "blood." Spread throughout were certain emotional elements focused on hostility to civilization, among which were the German Romantics as well as such luminaries as Wagner and Nietzsche. Finally, reflecting the mood of the times, were the strong undercurrents of nationalist and socialist ideas, tied in with anything that could be thrust into the grab bag that was National Socialism. "We gathered our ideas from all the bushes along side our life's road," Hitler once stated, " and we no longer know where they come from."[121]

For Hitler, this ideology, apart from the overpowering drive for Eastern *Lebensraum* and *concomitant racial dominance*, was nothing more than the "great landscape painted on the background of our stage." As a result, contradictions and inconsistencies in the articles of faith were unimportant to him so long as they did not interfere with success, "the sole arbiter of right and wrong." This outlook was evident throughout his career when, on innumerable occasions, he jettisoned the so-called "granite" principles of National Socialism as soon as they became impediments to tactical considerations. There was, in fact, nothing the Nazi leader was not prepared to proclaim or abandon for the sake of gaining power even if it meant that he had to "swear six false oaths a day." "Any idea, even the best," he concluded in *Mein Kampf*, "becomes a danger when it imagines it is an end in itself, whereas in reality it represents merely a means to such."[122]

Underlying all this was the ideological link to the Nazi leader's "authority" or "rule," defined by Max Weber as power that is recognized by other people in any one of three ways. The first authority is that of the "eternal yesterday," derived from ancient custom and tradition. "My father was the king.... He is now dead. I am therefore King and you must obey me."

43

Rational-legal, the second authority, is basically expressed as: "I was elected...by legal and constitutional procedures, and therefore you must obey me...." Finally, there is the authority derived from an "extraordinary and personal gift of grace," which Weber called charisma, derived from the Greek word for spirit. "God...has laid His Hand upon me to make me the leader and therefore you must obey."[123]

It was this third authority that developed within the NSDAP during the *Kampfzeit*. And after the assumption of power by rational-legal means in 1933, National Socialism was revealed for what it had been since the emergence of the *Führerprinzip* in that period of struggle: the ideological justification of the Fürhrer as the ultimate source of truth and power with the concomitant requirement for absolute obedience, the basis of charismatic domination. This merger of ideology into the charismatic leader created a faith solely focused on Hitler.[124]

Key to this concept of charismatic *Führerprinzip* was the assertion of Hitler's infallibility which fed, as we have seen, into an ever-expanding sense of *destiny and hubris*. By the late 1930s, the Nazi leader began to believe that he was actually free from human error, his goals supported by the will of Providence. "When I look back upon the five years that lie behind us," he stated in the summer of 1937, "I can say, this was not the work of human hands alone."[125] The following year at the Nuremberg Party Rally, his followers proclaimed this to the world. For one high party official, the Nazi leader was the only human who had never made a mistake, while another compared him to God. But it was left to SS Gruppenführer Schulz from Pomerania to add the final touch by asserting that Hitler was greater than Christ, since the latter had been followed by only twelve disloyal disciples, while the former had a nation of seventy million loyal citizens behind him.[126]

This type of charismatic authority is also a reminder how such rule can further the "craziness" of states. For there is a need with such authority to maintain both in the ruling elites and among the people themselves the myth of the leader's unerring correct judgment and independence from factional disputes. Thus, in contrast to the massive unpopularity of the NSDAP and the daily greyness of life under Nazism as the

Third Reich wore on, there was Hitler's soaring popularity that stemmed, in part, from his image of a leader aloof from the daily realities of political and domestic life. It was an image, as we have seen, to which Hitler to some extent had to adjust, thus adding to a leadership style of aloof noninterference and a tendency always to side with "the big battalions."[127] This, in turn, fostered the need on the part of the Nazi leader to produce even greater achievements in order to bind the masses closer to the Führer and to prevent the "vitality" of the Third Reich from slipping into stagnation, disenchantment and probable collapse. This aspect played a major role in impelling the Nazi regime toward craziness, always impeding the establishment of a "state of normalcy"; promoting instead the same radical, essentially negative dynamism that had led to the social integration of the Nazi movement, but when applied to the international scene, could only lead to disaster.[128]

THE RATIONALITY OF IRRATIONALITY

"Irrational" reactions from leaders of crazy states are a common phenomenon. Thus, there is the picture of Libya's Gadhafi working himself into a paroxysm of rage in a television interview; or Saddam Hussein calmly outlining how he will defeat the United States. In many cases, however, such displays are nothing more than rational combinations of fanaticism and calculation. For example, if general conventional war is seen to be disastrous and essentially irrational, as it was in the 1930s by most states still reflecting on experience in World War I, then the state most able, like Hitler's Germany, to demonstrate a willingness to move closer to such a war is more likely to succeed in intimidation. "There is a rational advantage," Herman Kahn has pointed out in this regard, "to be gained from irrational conduct or from the expectations of irrational conduct."[129]

This so-called "rationality of the irrational" can thus be applied in an ends-means instrumental sense to the pure, value maximizing decision model. At the most basic level, as Thomas Schelling has noted, some inmates in mental institutions often seem to cultivate, deliberately or instinctively, value systems that cause them to be less susceptible to disciplinary threats and more capable of exercising coercion. Examples include a deliberately induced inability to hear or understand, or acquiring in the way of small children a reputation for frequent lapses of self-control that reduce or eliminate the deterrent effect of punishment. Even a careless or self-destructive attitude in terms of injury moves toward the rational construct of the model with the threat: "I'll cut a vein in my arm if you don't let me...." constituting a genuine strategic advantage. In Joseph Conrad's *The Secret Agent,* in this regard, a known anarchist with a container of nitroglycerin in his pocket is left unmolested by the London Police because he has threatened to blow himself up. A companion wonders why the police would believe anything so preposterous, to which the anarchist calmly replies:

> In the last instance it is character alone that makes for one's safety.... I have the means to make myself deadly, but that by itself, you understand, is absolutely nothing in the way of protection. What is effective is the belief those people have in my will to use the means. That's their impression. It is absolute. Therefore, I am deadly.[130]

Hitler had a firm understanding of this approach. After his father's death, for example, his mother attempted to have him continue his education at the *Realschule.* Not for the last time, the 13-year-old successfully imposed his will by means of an hysterical reaction in the form of an illness. "The goal for which I had so long silently yearned, for which I had always fought," he wrote of the incident in *Mein Kampf,* "had through this event suddenly become reality almost of its own accord."[131]

In a similar manner in later years, Hitler played upon his reputation as a *Teppichfresser,* a rug chewer given to ungovernable rages. This was particularly evident in his tirades against the Austrian Chancellor in February 1938 and the Czechoslovakian president in March of the following year, the latter almost succumbing to a weak heart in response to the verbal onslaught. At no time was the calculated irrationality of the Nazi leader better illustrated than in his August 23, 1939 meeting with the British Ambassador, at which, as we have seen, he was presented with a note from Chamberlain indicating Britain's readiness to honor its Polish guarantees while still holding out hope for negotiations. Hitler responded by working himself into a frenzy, launching a violent tirade against the British whom he held responsible for the crisis. "To all appearance," Alan Bullock has noted, "Hitler was a man whom anger had drawn beyond the reach of rational argument." And yet, as an official from the Wilhelmstrasse recorded that day: "Hardly had the door shut behind the Ambassador than Hitler slapped himself on the thigh, laughed and said: 'Chamberlain won't survive that conversation; his Cabinet will fall this evening.'"[132]

CHAPTER 7

GOALS AND ORGANIZATIONS

Foreign policy goals are the key ingredient in determining or examining crazy states. These goals can be revealed in many ways, ranging from a leader's official and semiofficial pronouncements to actual implementation. In terms of strategic analysis of crazy states, the primary focus is on those national goals which involve external aggression. These could vary from slight border incursions to an ideological crusade for converting entire regions, if not the world. An important corollary to all this, of course, is goal commitment. With what intensity and consistency, in other words, do policymakers pursue these goals? The answer can be found in the combination of the leader, who establishes the goals in accordance with his world view, and the governmental structure in which every leader, no matter how authoritarian the system, must play a functional role in terms of organizations and politics.[133]

CRAZY GOALS

In examining the goals of any leader as a means of finding some consistency in the course of that leader's foreign policy, it is necessary to guard against teleologically squaring the circle in interpreting results only in terms of those goals. Nevertheless, early goals or indications of a world view on the part of a political leader are good startpoints for any analysis. In Hitler's case, for instance, his ideological goals of *Lebensraum* and racial domination were clearly spelled out in *Mein Kampf* and in myriad speeches. How those goals were translated into reality forms the basis of most controversy on this subject, which in turn provides valuable insights into the progressive radicalization process that leads to the formation of a crazy state.

The "intentionalists" see the conquest of *Lebensraum* and racial domination as intrinsically related, programmatic components of Hitler's *Weltanschauung*, which formed the essence of the Nazi leader's politics. The "programmatic" concept has been complemented by studies on Hitler's so-called *Stufenplan* to expand German power in rationally calculated stages, beginning with the restoration of the Reich to great power status; followed by achieving a position of preeminence in Central Europe for Germany; leading then to continental hegemony and the acquisition of *Lebensraum* in the East by subjugating the USSR; and finally the triumphant march of this "Greater German Reich" on the road to global dominance.

None of these views is intended to indicate a definite timetable on the part of the Nazi leader, but to demonstrate, instead, the consistent driving force of these components, while acknowledging Hitler's ability to improvise and his great tactical flexibility.[134] Added to this picture of relentless consistency are studies of Hitler's role in domestic policy, in which the Nazi leader, working with tactical adroitness, moved in a logical and internally rational series of moves toward the attainment of total power in order to implement the ideological goals of his world view.[135]

The "functionalists" or "structuralists," on the other hand, focus on a picture of Darwinian rivalries preventing any full coordination by fractured governmental machinery to bureaucratize the Führer's charismatic authority. As a result, the Nazi leader's personal world view served, at least in part, a functional role by providing "directions for actions" *(Aktionsrichtungen)*, with Hitler not so much creating policy, as sanctioning pressures operating from different forces within the regime. In this construct, the pursuit of *Lebensraum* was nothing more than Hitler's need to maintain the dynamic momentum he had unleashed, which in turn created the need for complete freedom of action, only obtainable by breaking all diplomatic norms. In any event, the Nazi leader's foreign policy goals prior to 1939 were nebulous, unspecific and basically utopian with the goal of attaining *Lebensraum* being an ideological, metaphorical symbol that explained incessant foreign policy activity. That activity was used as a means of integrating and diverting antagonistic forces in the Reich brought about by the increased involvement of the masses. In this manner, the plebiscitary social dynamic in foreign policy exerted increasing pressure on Hitler and his regime to transform the *Lebensraum* metaphor into reality.[136]

In terms of the Jewish component, both schools are agreed that Hitler maintained throughout his political career a deep, pathologically violent hatred of Jews and that this paranoid obsession was a major factor in determining the climate within which the spiraling radicalization of anti-Jewish actions occurred. In this regard, it was Hitler in his capacity as head of the Third Reich whose fanaticism on the "Jewish Question" provided impulse, sanction and legitimation for the escalating horrors that eventually culminated in the "Final Solution." The "intentionalists," however, go beyond this to see unwavering continuity in Hitler's aim to destroy the Jews, his dominance in shaping anti-Jewish policy, and his decisive role in the initiation and implementation of the Holocaust. Lucy Dawidowicz, for instance, views the entire process as one long rational search on the part of the Nazi leader for the means to fulfill his goal of destroying Jewery—a goal which he had formed as early as 1918 and which was openly espoused as a program of annihilation in *Mein Kampf*. This program was to become "a blueprint" for his policies when he came to power. "There never had been any ideological deviation," Dawidowicz concludes. "In the end only the questions of opportunity mattered."[137]

The "functionalists" continue to see at least part of the Holocaust in organizational terms, focusing on the oddly fragmented decision-making process in Nazi Germany which resulted in improvised bureaucratic initiatives with their own internal momentum that led to the dynamics of cumulative radicalization. In this context, the key lay in the local exterminations in the East, stemming from the unexpected failure of the Blitzkreig invasion of the Soviet Union and the concomitant inability, after fall 1941, of Gauleiter, SS chiefs and other officials in the Occupied Territories to cope with the growing number of Jews in their domains as a result of breakdowns in the deportation plans. "It thus seems that the liquidation of the Jews began not solely as the result of an ostensible will for extermination," Martin Broszat has pointed out in this regard, "but also as a 'way out' of a blind alley into which the National Socialists had manoeuvred themselves. The practice of liquidations, once initiated and established, gained predominance and evolved in the end into a comprehensive 'programme.'"[138]

CRAZY REALITY

Any examination of deviations from the pure rationality model has to deal with the personal characteristics and intentions of the policymaker as well as the structure and process of decision making. In most cases there will not be a single focus. For example, in terms of Hitler's part in shaping anti-Jewish and foreign policy, the "intentions" of the Nazi leaders as well as the impersonal "structures" of the regime were both critical elements, though in varying degrees of mix. In the case of foreign policy, Hitler shaped initiatives and made the key decisions. In this regard, his ideological goals were important factors in the course that policy was to follow, but are often difficult to separate from strategic-power considerations and economic interests. Nevertheless, the force of Hitler's personality and his pragmatic goals can be seen throughout the foreign policy of the Third Reich.

At the same time, the charismatic function of the Führer role was also key to a foreign policy moving inexorably toward war, since it provided rational legitimization of the means towards the ends it was presumed were desired by the Nazi leader. This legitimization extended to the self-interest of the Army leadership, to the ambitions of the diplomats at the Wilhelmstrasse, and to the greed and ruthlessness of the industrialists. Equally important, the charismatic legitimization provided in the realm of foreign policy a chauvinistic and imperialistic basis for the party masses to clamor for the restoration of Germany's power and glory. In the end, it is the complex mixture of Hitler's ideological intentions combined with the conditions and forces that structured those intentions that explain the foreign policy of the Third Reich.

In the case of the "Jewish Question," Hitler's primary input was establishing the long-range goal, shaping the climate and sanctioning the increasingly radical actions of those around him who were acting in the name of his "heroic" charismatic intentions. The overall effect should not be underrated. The Nazi leader's obsession with *Lebensraum,* for instance, was tied to a reemergence of the Ottonions and Hohenstaufen feudal empires populated by a new master race of Ayrian blood—all of which would begin with the resumption of medieval colonialization. In this context, the East was to be considered initially an area like the "wild West," outside the bounds of law and order where a new "nobility of the sword," the Gauleiter, would be expected after 10 years, according to Hitler, "to be in a position to inform me that these regions have once again become German."[139]

In addition, there were the Nazi leader's public tirades of hate and vague threats against the Jews, the most notorious being his January 30, 1939 Reichstag speech in which he "prophesied" that the war would result *in the* "annihilation *(Vernichtung)* of the Jewish race in Europe." This was a prophesy to which he frequently referred during the war and which he postdated to the opening day of the conflict, reflecting his mental merger of that war and his "mission" to destroy the Jews.[140]

At the same time, the "Final Solution" was not just a product of the myriad "local initiatives" in the East which gained retroactive sanction "from above." There was also direction from the centers of power, primarily the Reich Security Head Office, but not from Hitler, although "undoubtedly the most important steps had his general approval and sanction."[141] What emerges from this is a picture of the Nazi leader who, despite his undeviating hatred of the Jews over the years, took little part in the overt formulation of anti-Jewish policy. Instead, his major role, as we have seen and as Ian Kershaw has noted,

> consisted of setting the vicious tone within whichthe persecution took place and providing the sanction and legitimation of initiatives which came mainly from others. More was not necessary. The vagaries of anti-Jewish policy both before the war and in the period 1939-41, out of which the 'Final Solution' evolved, belie any notion

of 'plan' or 'programme.' The radicalization could occur without any decisive steerage by Hitler. But his dogmatic, unwavering assertion of a vague ideological imperative — 'getting rid of the Jews' from Germany, then finding a 'final solution to the Jewish question' — which had to be translated into bureaucratic and executive action, was nevertheless the indispensable prerequisite for the escalating barbarity and the gradual transition into full-scale genocide.[142]

CHAPTER 8

EXTERNAL ACTION CAPABILITIES

In order for a crazy state to become a strategic problem, it must possess external action capabilities. Thus a deranged Soviet Union would have far greater significance than a small Third World country similarly affected. Figure 5 is a three-factor model with just some of the variables that shape such capabilities.[143]

The initial factor is concerned with a nation's infrastructure bearing on external action capabilities. The second factor includes realization variables which transform the infrastructure variables into external action capabilities, the dimensions of which form the third factor in the model and provide a breakdown into external action instruments. Each of the factors, of course, does not exist in a vacuum. Realization variables, for example, depend on, and to some extent in some situations, are even a function of the infrastructure variables. And infrastructure elements also depend in the long run on such realization variables as political capacity and national will. On the other hand, nuclear, biological and chemical weapons

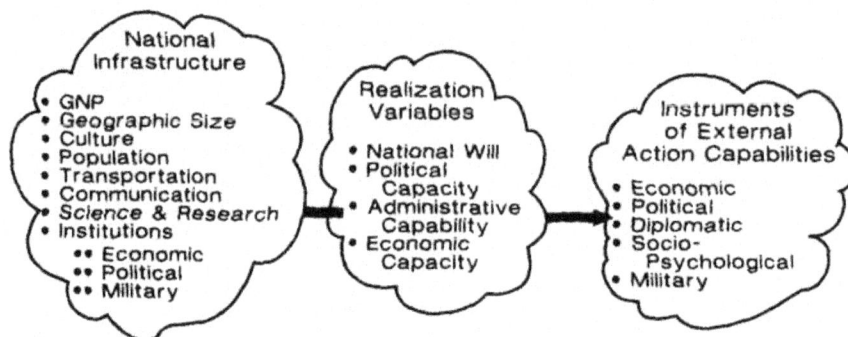

Figure 5. Capabilities for External Action.

or terrorist groups may provide external action capabilities out of proportion to the infrastructure of a relatively small state.[144]

In a pure rational model, the realization variables would operate perfectly, with the full potential of the external action infrastructure being realized. In reality, of course, in most nations there are significant deviations from the model. There may be an even greater tendency in this regard with crazy states if Nazi Germany is any indication. For as the political and ideological demands of the Nazi leaders came to play a dominant role in their alliance with Germany's military-industrial complex, instrumental rationality declined accordingly with a concomitant loss in ability to generate external action capabilities.[145]

REALIZATION VARIABLES — IRRATIONALITY IN PREPARATION

At the outset of the Nazi regime, the political decision was made to give absolute priority to rearmament. And yet there emerged over the years of peace many factors that inhibited the rational instrumental realization process that would have transformed resources efficiently into armaments. To begin with, there were the various interest groups with direct connections to Hitler in the charismatic chaos of the *Führerstaadt.* Party members were particularly onerous, often making it difficult for Hjalmar Schacht, the Minister of Economics, to cut public expenditures not associated with armaments. For example, in almost every instance when Schacht attempted to cut funds earmarked for municipal improvements, he was opposed by prominent Gauleiter and other party officials, all of whom could take the issues directly to the Nazi leader who invariably sided with them.[146]

Equally important in terms of rearmament was the regime's unwillingness to increase public expenditures and thus incur larger deficits which, it was believed, would destroy confidence in the government and lead to inflation. The fear of inflation, of course, was a holdover from previous non-Nazi governments that affected everybody from Hitler to Schacht, the latter a paragon of financial conservatism. For the Nazi leader, it was all simply a matter of control. "Inflation is lack of discipline—lack of discipline in the buyers and lack of discipline in the soldiers," he stated early on. "I will see to it that prices remain stable. That is what my S.A. is for."[147] In the end, the spectre of inflation was a major restraining influence on both the development of raw material industries and total military expenditures.

Added to all this was the inefficiency of the National Socialist regime in planning and implementing the war production program. There was, for instance, no central agency prior to the war for coordinating the material demands of the services of the armed forces. The result in terms of rearmament was that the services created and then pursued their own weapons and equipment programs with almost no coordination and, as a result, with interservice rivalry for scarce raw materials often being intense, if not vicious.

Goring's "Four-Year Plan" in 1936 did not alleviate the situation; and Hitler did not improve matters by sanctioning armaments programs that were far removed from reality. Thus, the programs proposed and approved by the Nazi leader in 1938-39 included a massive expansion of the Luftwaffe and the so-called "Z-Plan" for creating a large ship navy—both of which, if implemented, would have required an amount of crude oil reserves in excess of the total annual production in the world. How far removed from reality such planning could be for an individual service was demonstrated in the initial army force for Barbarossa of approximately 150 divisions, only 46 of which were fully provided with German equipment and arms, the remainder either operating with captured Czech and French materiel or deficient in such key items as antitank guns. "In the light of such evidence," Burton Klein has concluded in this regard, "it would be difficult to deny that a more rational and better executed program would have given the National Socialists larger rearmament."[148]

Finally, in terms of impediments to rearmament, there was the unwillingness of Hitler and his regime to ask civilians to lower consumption, demonstrated by the government's unwillingness in 1937 to cut food imports in order to increase those of raw materials. In actuality, no choice had to be made until 1936 on the question of *Kannon oder Butter*, since increased civilian consumption as well as rearmament could be achieved together by using unemployed resources. After that, however, the German economy was operating at almost full employment; and a large increase of expenditures for armaments would have required, at the very least, a sharp curtailment of some types of civilian goods production. That did not happen. And although shortages of such vital raw materials as iron and other ores repeatedly delayed armaments production in the late 1930s, the volume of imported foodstuffs and textiles actually rose steadily during that period—all permitted by the regime in order to satisfy public demand, upon which, despite its use of terror, the government believed its stability and popularity rested. In these circumstances, major armament increases in the latter part of the decade overburdened economic capabilities while producing bottlenecks in all sectors of the economy as well as latent inflation. The armament achievements were considerable, but they were obtained at the expense of growing economic instability, while still falling short of the goals in Hitler's strategic plans.[149]

The concern with public well-being is a paradoxical development in an authoritarian, nondemocratic government, which, depending on the background of the leader and the culture of the population, could prove to be an important focus in examining a crazy state's ability to generate external action capabilities. Certainly it is key to understanding the Nazi leader's impact on the realization variables that affected such capabilities in the Third Reich. In his case, it began with the 1918 November revolution in Germany. And although in Hitler's version of the *Dolchstoss*, the so-called "stab in the back" that caused the revolution, there was no mention of the social and economic causes for that upheaval, he was acutely aware of them. "Clearly there was dire misery everywhere," he wrote in *Mein Kampf* of a leave spent in Berlin in the last year of the war. "The big city was suffering from hunger. Discontent was great."[150] And in his unpublished book in 1928, the Nazi leader stressed the need not to allow the living standards of "people of a definite cultural capacity" to decline.

> The broad masses especially will show no understanding of this. They feel the hardship; either they grumble against those who in their opinion are responsible—something which is dangerous...since thereby they provide the reservoir for all attempts at revolutionary upheavals—or through their own measures they try to bring about a rectification....[151]

As a consequence, the domestic policies of the Nazi regime swung inconsistently back and forth between vicious attacks on personal and political rights, on the one hand, and fearful circumspection inspired by the need to gain and maintain popularity with the masses on the other. At the same time, there was a disinclination on the part of the regime to require sacrifices from the population, demonstrated by the government's rejection of higher taxes as an alternative to deficit spending, its unwillingness in 1937 to cut food imports in order to increase raw material imports, and its failure to move workers out of nonessential occupations. All this culminated in 1938 when, despite pleas from the Ministry of Food and Agriculture, Hitler would not raise food prices for fear of the effect on living standards as well as worker morale. "How can I expect to wage war," he asked, "if I drive the masses into the same state of apathy that they were in during 1917-1918?"[152]

REALIZATION VARIABLES — IRRATIONALITY IN EXECUTION

Hitler's concern with any threat to "social peace" continued to affect the realization of external action capabilities throughout World War II. During the first months of that conflict, for instance, he withdrew plans for labor mobilization after workers protested the impact that such a move would have on wages, working conditions and living standards. In a similar manner as the war went on, other aspects of "business as usual" included the high level of consumer goods until 1943; the personal allowances paid to the wives of the military, which were so generous that most married women could not be persuaded to take up industrial work when that was belatedly sanctioned for women; and finally the incessant propaganda stressing that final victory was just around the corner, making sacrifice and effort appear less necessary. In all this, Hitler's concerns were the dominant factor. "For there is no doubt about it," he stated in 1942 while emphasizing the need to bring captured grain from the Soviet Union, "the morale of the people is dependent to quite a considerable degree on a sympathetic understanding of and catering for the little things that make life more pleasant for them."[153]

The Nazi leader's doubts about the solidarity of his regime continued up to the end to affect adversely Germany's ability to generate external action capabilities. In the spring of 1945, all ministers agreed that a drastic increase in taxation was necessary for combatting inflation and reducing civilian purchasing power. Hitler signed an order for this increase, but insisted that it should only be enacted when the German military won a victory. The tax increase was never put into effect. For Albert Speer, facing this defect in rational instrumentality on a daily basis, it was:

> one of the oddities of this war that Hitler demanded far less from his people than Churchill and Roosevelt did from their respective nations. The discrepancy between the total mobilization of labor forces in democratic England and the casual treatment of this question in authoritarian Germany is proof of the regime's anxiety not to risk any shift in the popular mood. The German leaders were not disposed to make sacrifices themselves or to ask sacrifices of the people. They tried to keep the morale of the people in the best possible state by concessions.... Whereas Churchill promised his people only blood, sweat, and tears, all we heard during the various phases and various crisis of the war was Hitler's slogan: 'The final victory is certain.'[154]

Another aspect of the wartime realization variables for Germany involved the twin goals of *Lebensraum* and the destruction of the Jews. That these goals were "crazy" is an almost universal judgment. But there is another component of this issue that brings it full circle to the question of whether rationality can go beyond instrumentality and also apply to goals. The final solution against the Jews was initiated on a large scale in the summer of 1941 at the same time that the final solution of Hitler's grand design in foreign policy, the war against the Soviet Union, was undertaken. At that same moment, as the blueprints of Hitler's foreign and racial policies reached their climaxes, the inevitable struggle for priorities between the two began. To have discontinued temporarily the persecution of the Jews in the summer of 1941 and concentrated all means on the conquest of living space, or vice versa, was not possible for the Nazi leader whose policies, as Eberhard Jäckel has pointed out, "took their course with an obstinate, brutal, and final self-destructive consistency."[155] Thus, Hitler's goals were irrational in the limited meaning of choosing mutually conflicting ends—in the sense, for instance, that mankind's insistence on using up the Earth's resources as quickly as possible in order to maximize self-interest is irrational.[156]

Hitler's Jewish policy was also profoundly irrational in an instrumental sense in terms of external action capability. For the most part in the early stages of that policy, there was no contradiction between the objectives of the relatively autonomous SS and the interests of the German capitalists. The latter was quite willing to take advantage of the Jewish labor concentrated in the Polish ghettos and the lack of restrictions concerning the total exploitation of this labor for minimal cost. But with the huge extension of the "Jewish Question" in the Occupied Territories and the move into the final solution accompanying the increased labor shortage of the Third Reich, the radical nihilism of National Socialism emerged triumphant over "rational" economic interest. This was illustrated by the initial extermination of Polish Jews, thousands of whom were skilled metal workers from Polish arms factories. And although the Nazis continued to use some Jewish labor almost to the war's conclusion, the regime also used on a continuous basis the scarce transport equipment to move human cargo across Europe to extermination points—all at a time when German forces were desperate for resupplies and when German industry was desperate for manpower.[157]

This irrationality extended down to the "normal" concentration camps, initially created to neutralize the internal enemies of the Reich and later used to provide forced labor. At these camps, the SS was unable to preserve the physical fitness of the prisoners marked for such labor because of inadequate food, barbarous working conditions and totally

61

deficient housing and hygiene. Nor could threats of punishment in such cases increase productivity. The average work done by concentration camp inmates, Speer estimated in this regard, amounted to only one-sixth of that achieved by free civilian labor. "In short," one historian summed up the fundamental irrationality, "it turned out that a system based on repression, dehumanization and physical extermination could hardly be converted into a high-productivity economic enterprise."[158]

WEAPONS OF MASS DESTRUCTION

Hitler's involvement in the invention of new weapons had mixed results. On the one hand, when his interest was aroused in any piece of technology like the V-1 flying bomb or the V-2 rocket, his energy and enthusiasm, focused through his dominant decision-making position, could quickly impel a developmental project to the top of any priority list. On the other hand, the Nazi leader's lack of discipline coupled with his initial enthusiasm for new weapons resulted in a total lack of prioritization which meant, in turn, that Germany suffered from an excess of "secret weapons" throughout the war. For example, his commitment to the huge V-2 rocket was, as David Irving has noted, "an extravagant irrelevance" that siphoned off a large amount of industrial capacity which could have been used in manufacturing more mundane and useful weapons such as the surface-to-air rocket, first developed in 1942. That weapon, with its ability to hit enemy bombers at 50,000 feet, as Speer pointed out, might have beaten back the 1944 Allied spring air offensive, particularly if it had been combined with the new jet fighter, its development also a victim of Hitler's interference.[159]

As a consequence of all this, German scientists were deeply involved in the political process, with the life of projects often dependent on the most outrageous whims of the Führer or his inner circle. Under these circumstances, it was almost impossible for the scientists, whose expertise was supposed to be in either rational calculation or the analysis of data designed to aid rational calculation, to be distinguished from the party politicians who gained their official status based on entirely different criteria. Many scientists simply retreated into their own world, conducting investigations and experiments with no possible application to the war effort, despite the Nazi slogan: "German science in the cause of war." The head of the uranium project, for instance, did not hesitate to use funds and special privileges accorded that project in the expectation of some military benefit, for the general furthering of German theoretical science. "Academically a very satisfying pursuit," David Irving has pointed out, "it was not the way to win wars."[160]

Nevertheless, German scientists in the Nazi era made many scientific breakthroughs with military applications, one of the most significant of which was Tabun, a new nerve gas that penetrated the filters of all known gas masks and produced fatalities after even limited contact.[161] Why Hitler did not use this and other gases can only be a matter of conjecture. Certainly there was his own experience in a gas attack before Ypres on October 13, 1918, from which he "stumbled and tottered back with burning eyes."[162] And there was always the abysmal German intelligence trumpeting the chemical warfare edge of the Western allies that blinded the Nazi leader to Germany's unique advantage with nerve gas. Or perhaps he realized that at the tactical and operational level, where he increasingly retreated as the war went on, chemical warfare was of as dubious value as at the strategic level.[163]

What is certain is that Hitler generally opposed the offensive use of gas, despite some consideration of its use during the war, and that he was concerned about allied retaliation. How concerned he was on this matter was demonstrated by the fact that he prohibited the transfer of any gas munitions outside the pre-war Reich borders for fear of accidental use. And as German forces retreated on both fronts in the closing months of the war, there was the personal order over his signature that no toxic chemical dumps were to be blown up in case such actions might be construed as initiation of gas warfare. But if the costs were so great that even Hitler could see the irrational ends-means disconnect, it should not be forgotten that where poison gas could be used without this cost, it was, as millions of genocidal victims attest.[164]

63

Nuclear weapons, however, were another matter. In June 1942, Speer discussed the German uranium project with Hitler as one item on a long agenda. No other documentary evidence exists to show the Nazi leader's involvement in that project, although there are indications that he certainly would have approved the construction of an atomic bomb if he had been convinced of its feasibility. He was interested, for example, in the most advanced conventional explosives, once boasting that the V-1 flying bomb used an explosive "2.8 times as powerful as normal bomb explosives."[165] And there were vague allusions to atomic weapons in a talk with the Rumanian leader in August 1944, when Hitler described the most recent work on "new explosives whose development has been advanced to the experimental stage," adding that in his view the leap from modern explosives to the new development was the biggest since the invention of gunpowder. Moreover, when the subject turned to such secret weapons as the V-2 rocket, the Nazi leader pointed out that "another of these weapons...has such colossal force that all human life is destroyed within three or four kilometers of its point of impact..."[166]

By that time, the matter had long since been decided by a number of factors. To begin with, Hitler's anti-Semitic policies had depleted the ranks of nuclear scientists in his regime early on; and the entire atomic bomb effort still had Jewish associations in the mind of the Nazi leader who occasionally referred to nuclear physics as "Jewish physics."[167] Then there was the drafting of scientists into the Wehrmacht which increased so markedly by 1943 that one professor associated with the Reich Research Council warned that "while 3,000 fewer soldiers would not weaken the armed forces, 3,000 more physicists might well decide the war."[168] Most importantly, the German uranium project was directed by scientists throughout its existence, not by the military as was the case in the United States with the Manhattan Project. Acting alone, the nuclear scientists consistently failed to impress the Nazi leaders with anything but what Field Marshal Milch called their "artlessness and naivete."[169] As a result, the rapport between the scientists and the elites of government and industry, so necessary for the full and expeditious implementation of the nuclear program, was never established.[170]

All this notwithstanding, the German uranium project would have been a very near thing if it had not been for allied commando attacks in Norway on the German production of heavy water, the key ingredient for the type of reactors being researched in Berlin. The February 1943 raid on the Vemork facility east of Oslo was a conspicuous success, resulting in the loss of a ton of heavy water and the temporary closing of the plant. Such attacks, culminating a year later in the sinking of a Norwegian ferry with large supplies of heavy water, played the dominant role in ending German hopes of building an atomic reactor, much less an atomic bomb. How effectively the heavy water could have been used in Berlin was indicated by the Chief of the U.S. Scientific Intelligence Mission who inspected the underground uranium reactor bunker constructed to hold the first pilot reactor. "It looked as if it had once been excellently equipped," he wrote in July 1945. "I remembered the primitive setup with which Enrico Fermi had started in a basement room at Columbia University. By contrast, this Berlin laboratory, even empty, gave an impression of high-grade achievement."[171]

CHAPTER 9

THE WAY AHEAD

"Probably none of us is entirely 'normal,'" Hitler noted rather plaintively in 1941.[172] This, of course, is true. It is also true that all crazy states are not equally crazy. But by using the factors identified in the "black box" of Nazi Germany as a referent, the extent of a nation's craziness can be roughly identified.

To begin with, authoritarian, nondemocratic rule in a nation state is more likely to produce craziness from a Western democratic perception. Add charismatic, one-man rule, as was the case in Nazi Germany, or charismatic, collective rule, as is the case of the Mullah-led theocracy in Iran, and the stage is set for varying degrees of craziness. All this, in turn, depends on the impact such rule has on decision-making variables involved with bureaucratic organizations, governmental politics and the personal characteristics of the leader. In this construct, the operational code of any leader, but particularly one "touched by God," is extremely important. How such a leader views the world must be the logical startpoint. In this regard, as we have seen in the detrius of Hitler's mind, early speeches or writings by a leader as well as psychoanalytical studies can provide some insight into his cognitive trail, touching on such factors as ethnocentrism, threat perception and long-term goals.

In particular, a leader's goals and his commitment to them are important dimensions of craziness, especially if the leader is, like Hitler, one of those "terrible simplifiers" of ideas.[173] At one end of the scale might be goals that do not go much beyond the status quo; or commitment that requires no more than minor parts of the budget and limited manpower being devoted to external goals, which in turn are subordinated to internal ones. The other end would involve extreme external goals up to the destruction of another nation state and the absorption or liquidation of its population. Or, in terms of commitment, an all-out devotion of resources to external goals, with internal objectives only perceived as means for external ends; and with the acceptance of these external goals perceived as a national mission up to the ultimate readiness to sacrifice national existence to achieve them.

This craziness intensifies, as we have seen in Hitler's Germany, if such a commitment is focused through charismatic authority derived from neo-feudal personal loyalty. When that authority is superimposed upon the bureaucratic structures of a modern nation state, the corrosive effect on those structures leaves the power of the state intact for the pursuit of crazy goals while destroying institutional restraints. The result is progressive and cumulative radicalization of a regime in which more and more power resides with the leaders and the loyal paladins of his inner circle.

This type of organization can only feed the ego and hubris of the leaders perched at the very top. A Kim Il Sung or a Saddam Hussein, in this regard, is no more likely to suffer adversarial inputs into his decision-making process than Hitler. In the case of Hussein, for instance, there is the story of a Cabinet meeting held in the dark summer of 1982 when Iraq was bracing for an Iranian invasion. At that meeting, the Minister of Health suggested that the Iraqi ruler resign temporarily from office in order to facilitate a negotiated cease fire. Hussein demonstrated no sign of irritation, offering instead to discuss the matter with the minister in another room. Shortly after they left, a shot was heard, and the Iraqi President returned alone to the Cabinet showing no sign that anything had happened. The issue of his resignation was not raised again.[174]

All this can affect a leader's propensity to take risks, an important dimension of craziness. It is a dimension that brings the analysts full circle back to the cognitive trail of the crazy state leader, since, as was the case at times with Hitler, what is deemed risky by other nations and even by internal military and diplomatic elite, may not be so perceived by the leader. To be aware of cultural and/or perceptual differences on the part of a crazy state leader, however, does not lessen the importance of this subjective factor in evaluating craziness. At one extreme are "normal" leaders who tend to avoid risky policies. At the other extreme, there could be the preference for particularly risky policies that might vary from ideological commitment to adventurism and risktaking as preferable life styles. That these are key considerations in examining a leader like Saddam Hussein is self-evident. What makes the Iraqi President even more dangerous, some analysts have pointed out in this regard, is that rather than compromise or retreat when he encounters problems as a result of running risks, he tends to double his bets.[175]

Risk perception, as we have seen, has a great deal to do with instrumental rationality. Total irrationality in the sense of a complete rejection of the need to relate ends to means is rarely encountered even in the craziest of national leaders. In the early stages of his career before succumbing to the nemesis of hubristic success, Hitler adjusted to mistakes like the 1923 putsch which resulted from an imbalance in the means-ends relationship. And in 1939 with the Nazi-Soviet Nonaggression Pact, the Nazi leader was willing to jettison fundamental ideological animosities to further means-ends commensurability. More recently, in the fall of 1990, Saddam Hussein demonstrated a similar rational tendency with the Iraqi-Iranian Pact, by which the Iraqi leader returned most of the territory acquired in the savage 8-year war with Iran in order to ensure the security of Iraq's border with that country. Finally, there is the picture of Hitler during the later stages of World War II retreating into cognitive dissonance or down to a lower level of warfare when faced by too large an irrational gap at the strategic level between means and ends.

In the end, all these factors for evaluating craziness overlap with a leader's style. At the personal level, as Hitler's nonbureaucratic habits demonstrated, decision-making style may affect the entire functioning of government. In terms of the international arena, style may reflect the no-holds-barred, *coup de main*, revolutionary type approach that is part of the normal path to power for leaders within the type of parties that seek to gain national dominance by other than rational-legal means.

At its most extreme form of craziness, this factor can encompass a complete rejection of diplomatic norms and the adoption of methods that could include eco-terrorism, mass assassination of opposing leaders, systematic sabotage, counter-value terror—all the way up to genocide as a style of operation. Strategies, in turn, will incorporate these stylistic methods, depending on external action capabilities. For example, the socio-psychological instrument of external action, as the Nazis effectively demonstrated, lends itself to deception and fifth column-type infiltration and erosion from within—the latter to the extent that the name of the Norwegian fascist, Vidkum Quisling, has passed into the English language as a synonym for such activity. On the other hand, a nuclear capability may cause a crazy state to adopt strategies ranging from blackmail to occupation or destruction of neighboring states.

THE MUNICH METAPHOR

Containment is not the strategic answer to crazy states, since it is based on an assumption that if foreign policy successes are denied aggressive nations, then domestic constituencies will insist on change and thus moderate expansion. Although it appears that this "cure" may have worked for the Soviet Union after 45 years, an increasingly multipolar world in an era of advanced weapons technology is simply too dangerous to wait for crazy state constituencies to rise up against the pervasive terror that normally forms a part of the authoritarian rule in such states.

The inner logic of such terror was revealed in 1956 at the 20th Congress of the Soviet Communist Party, when Nikita Khrushchev revealed for the first time the full scope of Stalin's atrocities. As the premier spoke, one account goes, he received a note passed up from the audience. Khrushchev glanced at the note and then read it aloud: "If Stalin was such a monster, why didn't you and the Soviet leadership stand up to him?" The Soviet leader added: "This is an excellent question. I would be grateful if the comrade who asked it would rise so that I can answer him face to face." There was no movement in the auditorium. "Well," Khrushchev finished, "there's the answer to your question."[176]

Unlike containment, deterrence assumes no cure for an aggressive nation—a much more realistic method of dealing with crazy states. Concessions to an aggressive state, according to this model, sometimes named after the 1938 Munich Conference, simply lead that state to expect further concessions. In opposition, the so-called "spiral" model looks to the outbreak of World War I and focuses on the security perceptions of the other state, arguing that correctly executed concessions to another state lead to reciprocation from that state. Perceptions of friendship can become, in other words, self-fulfilling prophecies given enough time and the right environment. Thus, there is the British Ambassador to Germany cabling London in February 1939.

> My instinctive feeling is that this year will be the decisive one, as to whether Hitler comes down on the side of peaceful development and closer cooperation with the West or decides in favour of further adventures eastward.... If we handle him right, my belief is that he will become gradually more pacific. But if we treat him as a pariah or mad dog we shall turn him finally and irrevocably into one.[177]

This example demonstrates, of course, that the most obvious problem with the concession approach is when an aggressive state doesn't respond in kind to conciliation. In such instances, minor concessions—the willingness to treat individual problems separately, and even an offer for negotiations—can convince an aggressor that the status quo power is operating from a position of weakness. Moreover, as Hitler's foreign policy repeatedly demonstrated in the 1930s, once an aggressive state comes to believe in the weakness of the defenders of the status quo, it may be impossible to alter this image short of war.

Another particularly serious aspect of this problem is when nation A makes concessions to aggressive nation B in the incorrect belief that B is a status quo power. Such concessions are especially likely to be misinterpreted if B does not understand that A's policy is based on a false image of B. In this case, aggressive nation B will often think that its intentions

71

are obvious to A and, as a consequence, will conclude that any concessions made by A must be the product of fear and weakness.[178]

All this was evident with Hitler as the Munich Conference began to run its full course. At that time, the Nazi leader appeared to believe that the British were aware that his ambitions did not stop at the borders of areas inhabited by Germans. As a result, he concluded that Chamberlain's conciliatory efforts reflected not so much a feeling that Germany would be satiated by these concessions, but the fact that Britain lacked the resolve to go to war in order to oppose German hegemony on the Continent. Since Hitler did not perceive that Chamberlain's policy was based on an analysis of German intentions that was later altered by that country's seizure of non-German Czechoslovakia, the Nazi leader in September 1939 could not understand why British policy would be any different than it had been in September 1938.

The problem in all this was summed up by Nikoli Bukharin, the Communist ideologue up to the great purges in the mid-1930s. "Imperialism is a policy of conquest," he wrote. "But not every policy of conquest is imperialism."[179] In other words, there is a distinction between a policy of conquest operating within the existing status quo and one seeking to overthrow it. The distinction is not academic. "Appeasement is a foreign policy," Hans Morganthau has pointed out in this regard, "that attempts to meet the threat of imperialism with methods appropriate to a policy of the status quo."[180]

To make such a distinction in a given situation is extremely difficult, as we have seen in the case of Hitler. How could anyone gauge with any degree of certainty what his ultimate objectives were? From 1935 on, the Nazi leader piled demand upon demand, each of which taken by itself could be fully reconciled with a policy of status quo within adjustments of the Versailles territorial provisions; yet each of which might be a step on the path to empire. The individual moves in themselves were ambiguous and, as a result, did not reveal the actual nature of the policy of which they were components and which were best summarized in a confidential conversation by the Nazi leader during this period. "The

72

struggle against Versailles," he said, "is the means, but not the end of my policy. I am not in the least interested in the former frontiers of the Reich. The recreation of pre-war Germany is not a task worthy of our revolution."[181]

The distinction is too fine for the modern world. As soon as a state begins to exhibit some of the characteristics of craziness, deterrence should be used to ensure not only that the state does not commit aggression, but that it does not significantly improve its external action capabilities. In order for this concept to work, there has to be at least a modicum of instrumental rationality on the part of the nation to be deterred. Absent this, deterrence factors such as fear and uncertainty would be irrelevant, since they suggest consequences—a link between means and ends. But such extremes, as demonstrated for most of the peacetime history of the Third Reich, hardly ever obtain even in the craziest of states.

At the same time, there should be some appreciation of the fundamental values of a crazy state, no matter how bizarre in Western perceptions, if there is to be effective deterrence. Without this appreciation, deterrence may be attempted by threatening punishment directed at values which, while important to the deterring nation, may be quite irrelevant to the crazy state. A boycott threat, for example, might be viewed as welcome aid by a crazy state leader in isolating his country from outside influence while concurrently increasing the threat perception of the general population. Even limited military threats may help such a state mobilize its population by confirming the image of the external world that its leader wants the people to have.

In all this, credibility remains a key ingredient of deterrence that will have to be achieved through obvious actions which cannot be ignored even by highly-biased, ideologically-shaped perceptions of what constitutes reality. The consequences of not being deterred, in other words, must not be perceived by a crazy state as just possible or even highly probable. Those consequences must be assured, particularly if there is a high propensity for risk on the part of the nation to be deterred. In such cases, Thomas Schelling's concepts of clear thresholds and automated reactions in a conventional sense might apply,

73

with visible, irreversible commitments to undertake clearly defined actions in clearly defined circumstances. In such circumstances, at some point in the buildup of deterrence forces, no matter where a state lies on the spectrum of craziness and no matter how great the differences in culture and mindset, attention must finally be paid, as Willy Loman's wife reminds the world in *Death of a Salesman*. "It is sometimes stated," Herman Kahn has pointed out in this regard,

> that even an adequate...deterrent would not deter an irrational enemy. This might be true if irrationality were an all-or-nothing proposition. Actually, irrationality is a matter of degree and if the irrationality is sufficiently bizarre, the irrational decision maker's subordinates are likely to step in. As a result, we should want a safety factor in...deterrence systems so large as to impress even the irrational and irresponsible with the degree of their irrationality and therefore the need for caution.[182]

THE VIETNAM METAPHOR

The Vietnam experience has left two major lessons that are important in dealing with crazy states if deterrence fails. The first is that if action is decided upon, there should be clear purposes and definable military objectives. "No one starts a war," Clausewitz pointed out, "...without first being clear in his mind what he intends to achieve by that war and how he intends to conduct it."[183] The second lesson is that if ends are clear, means must serve them without succumbing to gradualism, or war by degree, as occurred in Vietnam. That conflict confirmed Clemenceau's observation that war is too serious to be left to generals in the Clausewitzian sense that military means must be governed by the political ends to which they are applied. But Vietnam also added the codicil that war is too serious to be left to the politicians in the sense that when ends are established, the military means must be used in a professional and decisive manner.[184]

Added to all this in terms of crazy states is the need to recognize their nature early on and to take direct action even before they become a visible threat. This imperative, in turn, may require that traditional approaches in international relations be jettisoned or, at the very least, altered. This applies particularly to the concept of national sovereignty, since most strategies to limit the growth of undeterrable crazy states may require, at one extreme, intervention in the domestic affairs of these countries. For example, external support for the German military conspirators in the late 1930s, before Hitler's foreign policy successes undermined their resolve and efforts, might have altered the course of events in Nazi Germany. At the other extreme, strategies against crazy states may require the outright destruction of particularly dangerous potential external action capabilities in peacetime, as was accomplished in the 1981 Israeli bombing of the Osiraq reactor, the wartime analogue of which was the Vemork heavy water raids in 1943-44.[185]

For the United States, however, it is more likely in the near future that military action against a crazy state will be conducted after that state has committed an act of aggression or, as in the limited case of Libya in 1986, an act of terrorism. Moreover, as the war with Hitler's Germany and the Gulf conflict both illustrate, such full-scale fighting against a crazy state is no different in most respects than war with a "normal" foe, given the usual problems ranging from coalition maintenance and strategy at the highest level to "beans and bullets" necessities at the lowest. Irrational fanaticism and martyr tendencies, of course, constitute important differences; but where the fighting actually occurs, a manifestation of these tendencies, such as human wave attacks, cannot stand up to modern technology as the Japanese learned in World War II and the Chinese in Korea. At the highest level of political-military decision making, however, crazy tendencies can have a vital impact in terms of ending the war.

The process of conflict termination can be superimposed on top of the pure rationality model, with all belligerents as unitary actors acting on all necessary information to make the proper cost-benefit calculations concerning the decision to end a war. "As war is no act of blind passion, but is dominated by the political objective," Clausewitz summed up the instrumental rationality of this approach,

> therefore the value of that objective determines the measure of sacrifices by which it is to be purchased...not only as regards

extent, but also as regards duration. As soon, therefore, as the required outlay becomes so great as that the political object is no longer equal in value, the object must be given up, and peace will be the result.[186]

The reality, of course, is much different, particularly in the case of crazy states where a leader's *Weltanschauung* may completely govern events. In victory, for instance, behavior may vary from Hitler's establishment of Vichey France to his brutal occupation of Poland or Hussein's similar treatment of occupied Kuwait. In defeat, there can be an all-encompassing success through failure, a last stand approach. "Remember," one Arab analyst has pointed out in this regard, "all our heros were defeated but brave."[187]

In a similar manner, there is the familiar romantic, *Götterdämmerung*-like vision of conflict termination associated with Hitler. Key to that vision was national resistance until the final *Untergang* of an undeserving nation, a belief to which Hitler held with remarkable consistency. "Unfortunately," he wrote in 1925, "the military defeat of the German people is not an undeserved catastrophe, but the deserved chastisement of eternal retribution. We more than deserved this defeat."[188] And 20 years later in the closing days of the war, the Nazi leader again returned to this theme. "If the war is to be lost, the nation will also perish," he stated, adding that "...it is better to destroy it and to destroy it ourselves."[189]

Nevertheless, there is a danger in allowing Hitler's vision to dominate an analysis of anticipated behavior by the leader of a crazy state in the face of military defeat. Apparently irrational resistance, for example, may be nothing more than holding out for better terms or until the situation changes. How else to explain the British resistance in 1940 against overwhelming odds before the United States and the Soviet Union had entered the war; or the Russian defense in late 1941 with German troops on the outskirts of Moscow.[190]

Moreover, there is evidence that within his own cognitive construct, no matter how far that construct was removed from reality, Hitler had rational reasons for delaying the end of the war. To begin with, there was the hope that his "miracle"

76

surprise weapons could turn the tide—a hope, as we have seen, unfulfilled because of the instrumentally irrational impact of his leadership on the generation of external action capabilities. Added to this was the expectation that the allied Grand Alliance would fall apart, that sooner or later the English-speaking Allies would join with Germany to keep the Soviet "invaders" out of Europe. "We'll fight," he stated in August 1944 in this regard, "until we get a peace which secures the life of the German nation...." And later that same day, the Nazi leader rationally weighed the political-military variables that might allow such an outcome. "The time hasn't come for a political decision," he concluded, adding that "...it is childish and naive to expect that at a moment of grave military defeats the moment for favorable political dealing has come. Such moments come when you are having success."[191]

THE SUMMING UP

The picture of Hitler at the end is not that of a raging maniac as was sometimes portrayed by his generals, but instead of a man roughly in control of his senses, making reasoned calculations.[192] There was, for example, his prescient view in his last testament in April 1945 of the postwar world. "With the defeat of the Reich and pending the emergence of the Asiatic, the African, and perhaps the South American nationalisms," he stated, "there will remain in the world only two Great Powers capable of confronting each other—the United States and Soviet Russia. The laws of both history and geography will compel these two powers to a trial of strength, either military or in the fields of economies and ideology."[193] To point all this out is in no way a vindication of the Nazi leader; rather it is a stronger indictment, for as Martin van Creveld has pointed out, "a maniac is not responsible for his actions. Hitler was."[194]

This picture of the Nazi leader also demonstrates how mixed the signals can be from a crazy state. Here again, the Munich analogy is a reminder of how difficult it is for nations, much less collective security organizations like the League of Nations, to come to agreement on the nature or even the existence of a threat from a crazy state. The lesson from the Gulf conflict, in this regard, is that obvious aggression must already have occurred by a crazy state and involve key strategic resources before global action is taken—and even then only with determined U.S. leadership. That this pattern is not the optimal way to deal with crazy states in the future is self-evident, particularly when a score or more of potentially crazy nations are already or becoming major military powers just as both superpowers are declining in conventional strength.[195]

All this suggests preventive action while the crazy state is in *status nascendi*. But in terms of collective security, there is no reason to expect that the United Nations will be any more successful in coming to agreement on the ambiguous signals of early craziness than its predecessor. If anything, with the proliferation of states and the decline of international standards of behavior in the post-World War II era, the United Nations is likely to be more tolerant of early signs of craziness in a particular nation.

Superpower cooperation is certainly a possibility, particularly in terms of taking the joint lead in enforcing the nonproliferation of nuclear, biological and chemical weapons technology. But a *Pax Americana - Sovietica* will hardly be a panacea. Superpower amity has little effect on regional enmity, as continuing problems in the Middle East demonstrate. And there is always the question of whether the Soviet Union, buffetted by internal fragmentation and societal upheavals, may not emerge in the future as a gigantic crazy state.

In the end, the United States will have to continue to take the lead in terms of setting the pattern in the post-cold war era for dealing with crazy states. Part of that effort will involve building up global or regional coalitions specifically targeted on crazy or rogue nations. These coalitions might focus on preventing the conditions which spawn such states, or on ensuring the cessation of imports that might improve their external action capabilities. The most important ingredient in these organizations will be deterrence—the obvious and credible willingness to use military power to prevent the growth and expansion of crazy states. The lesson from Vietnam, as we have seen in this regard, is not that this element of power

78

has little utility in the modern world, but that it has to be used with other power elements as an instrumentally rational link to clearly defined political objectives.

Future cutbacks in U.S. military capabilities will make it harder to maintain that link in dealing with crazy states. Nevertheless, the effort will have to be made. The problem of crazy states will not disappear. There will always be leaders like Hitler, able to bring a kind of rational order to their nations based on force, action and brutality, while ignoring the basic fabric of their own societies. For the majority of their populations, as it was for the citizens of Nazi Germany, this ordered framework will be enough even absent the societal fabric. The relationship between the strands that make up that fabric have grown too complicated in modern societies; and the great simplifiers in the tradition of Adolf Hitler stand ready in potential crazy states to abandon the weaving of these strands into a meaningful whole, slicing instead through the Gordian knot to offer apparent answers to what seem otherwise insoluble problems.

ENDNOTES

1. Henry Kissinger, *A World Restored*, Gloucester, MA: Peter Smith, 1964, pp. 2-3. Robert Jervis, *Perception and Misperception in International Politics*, Princeton: Princeton University Press, 1976, p. 271.

2. Joseph Frankel, *The Making of Foreign Policy. An Analysis of Decision Making*, London: Oxford University Press, 1968, p. 171. "In the nineteen-thirties Hitler established his position by a series of carefully planned movements," Eden wrote Eisenhower during the Suez crisis. "...Similarly the seizure of the Suez Canal is, we are convinced, the opening gambit in a planned campaign...." Fred C. Ikle, *How Nations Negotiate*, New York: Harper & Row, 1964, p. 158. Looking back on the Korean War, Truman wrote:

> In my generation, this was not the first occasion when the strong had attacked the weak. I recalled some earlier instances: Manchuria, Ethiopia, Austria. I remembered how each time that the democracies failed to act it had encouraged the aggressors to keep going ahead. Communism was acting in Korea just as Hitler, Mussolini, and the Japanese had acted ten, fifteen, and twenty years earlier. I felt certain that if South Korea was allowed to fall Communist leaders would be emboldened to override nations closer to our own shores. If the Communists were permitted to force their way into the Republic of Korea without opposition from the free world, no small nation would have the courage to resist threats and aggression by stronger Communist neighbors. If this was allowed to go unchallenged it would mean a third world war, just as similar incidents had brought on the second world war.

Harry S. Truman, *Memoirs*, Vol. 2: *Years of Trial and Hope*, Garden City, NY: Doubleday, 1956, pp. 332-33.

3. David Halberstram, *The Best and the Brightest*. Greenwich, CT: Fawcett, 1973, p. 729. For British analogies to Hitler during the Falklands War, see Richard Ned Lebow, "Miscalculation in the South Atlantic: The Origins of the Falklands War," *Psychology and Deterrence*,

eds. Robert Jervis, Richard Ned Lebow, Janice Gross Stein, Baltimore: Johns Hopkins University Press, 1985, pp. 115-116.

4.   Ann Devroy, "Bush Denies Preparing the U.S. for War," *The Washington Post,* November 2, 1990, p. A1.   See also Charles Krauthammer, "Nightmare From the '30s," *Ibid.*. July 27, 1990, p. A27. George F. Will, "Tribes with Flags," *Ibid.,* August 8, 1990, p. A21. For a counterview, see Rowland Evans and Robert Novak, "Overkill on Saddam," *Ibid.,* August 8, 1990, p. A21.

5.   Donald Kaul, "We're still trying to stop Hitler," *The Carlisle Sentinel,* August 30, 1990, p. C3.

6.   Yehezkel Dror, *Crazy States. A Counterconventional Strategic Problem,* Lexington, MA: D.C. Heath and Company, 1971.

7.   For a similar model, see Yehezkel Dror, *Public Policymaking Reexamined,* Scranton, PA: Chander Publishing Company, 1968, p. 134. It should be noted that the pure rationality model implies a perfect strategy (in the game-theory sense) which, prior to any action being implemented, also includes a means for readjusting the policy to the extent that the predicted results require. Thus no feedback mechanism is required in pure rational policymaking. In the real world, however, where actual results often are significantly different from expected results, feedback is also necessary during and after policymaking ends and may even be continuous and iterative in order to revise policies and improve the process. *Ibid.,* p. 161. See also James G. March and Herbert A. Simon, *Organizations,* New York: John Wiley and Sons, Inc., 1958, pp. 137ff and James E. Dougherty and Robert L. Pfaltzgraff, Jr., *Contending Theories of International Relations,* New York: J.B. Lippincott Company, 1971, p. 331.   The model incorporates Max Weber's three criteria for rational decision making. See Max Weber, *The Theory of Social and Economic Organizations,* trans. A.M. Henderson and Talcott Parsons, New York: 1947. pp. 115-118 and *Methodology of the Social Sciences,* trans. E.A. Shils and H. Finch, Glencoe, IL: The Free Press, 1949, pp. 52-53.

8.   Weber, *Theory,* p. 92. Exceptions are some problems that are susceptible to quantification such as those concerning inventory or replacement policies. Dror, *Public Policymaking,* p. 133. See also G.H. Snyder. *Deterrence and Defense,* Princeton: Princeton University Press, 1961, p. 25, and Sidney Verba, "Assumptions of Rationality and Non-Rationality in Models of the International System," *The International System. Theoretical Essays,* eds. Klaus Knorr and Sidney Verba. 2nd printing. Princeton: Princeton University Press, 1969, p. 107.

9.   On ideology, see Seweryn Braler, *Stalin's Successes: Leadership. Stability and Change in the Soviet Union,* New York: Cambridge University

Press, 1980; on culture and national character, see Gabriel Almond, *The American People and Foreign Policy*, New York: Praeger, 1960.

10. Harold and Margaret Sprout, *Foundations of International Politics*, Princeton, NJ: Van Nostrand, 1966, and Nicholas J. Spykman, America's *Strategy in World Politics: The United States and the Balance of Power*, New York: Harcourt Brace, 1942.

11. Graham T. Allison, *Essence of Decision. Explaining the Cuban Missiles Crisis*, Boston: Little, Brown & Company, 1971, and Roger Hilsman, *The Politics of Policy Making in Defense and Foreign Affairs*, Englewood Cliffs, NJ: Prentice-Hall, Inc., 1987.

12. Carl von Clausewitz, *On War*, trans. Michael Howard and Peter Paret, Princeton: Princeton University Press, 1976, p. 605. Charles Reynolds, *The Politics of War. A Study of the Rationality of Violence in Inter-State Relations*, New York: St. Martin's Press, 1989, p. 69. Colonel (Ret) Arthur Lykke has schooled an entire generation of U.S. Army War College students on his ends-ways-means paradigm for analyzing strategy at any level. For the strategists, this conceptual approach offers a much more comprehensive way to examine strategic problems and risk than the normal ends-means terminology used in strategic literature in which "means" normally incorporates Lykke's use of "ways" and "means." Thus, the definition of strategy as the calculated relationship of ends and means is also in instrumental terms the definition of rationality. Strategy, then, if executed properly, is by definition rational. Arthur F. Lykke, "Defining Military Strategy," *Military Review*, Vol. LXIX, No. 5, May 1989, pp. 2-8.

13. Dror, *Crazy States*, p. 19. But see Reynolds, p. 49, who argues that as long as those entrails contributed to Caesar's reasoning, helping to connect means and ends in a commensurate patterns, the instrumental sense of rationality was present.

14. Ken Booth, *Strategy and Ethnocentrism*, New York: Holmes & Meier Publishing, Inc., 1979, p. 64.

15. "Muslim perceptions would be guided more by passions than by Western expectations of logic and rationality." Mowahid H. Shah, "Perils of War: A Muslim View," *Christian Science Monitor*, November 5, 1990, p. 18. Michael I. Handel, *The Diplomacy of Surprise. Hitler, Nixon, Sadat*, Cambridge: Center for International Affairs, Harvard University, 1981, pp. 92-93. Richard K. Betts, *Surprise Attack Lessons for Defense Planning*, Washington, DC: The Brookings Institution, 1982, p. 130. Warfare is "an extension of culture, as well as of politics." Booth, p. 74. Reynolds, pp. 54, 56, and 90. It should be noted that a cultural failure to perceive what objectively is instrumental rationality on the part of one nation does not lessen that rationality. It is incumbent on other nations to move beyond ethnocentric limits if the rationality is to be appreciated.

16.   Roberta Wohlstetter, *Pearl Harbor: Warning and Decision*, Stanford: Stanford University Press, 1962, pp. 349 and 354.

17. Booth, p. 64.

18. Reynolds, p. 57; Frankel, p. 174.

19.   Abraham Kaplan, "Some Limitations on Rationality," *Rational Decision. Nomos VII. Yearbook for the American Society for Political and Legal Philosophy*, ed. Carl J. Friedrich, New York: Atherton Press, 1964, p. 57.

20. *Ibid.*

21. Felix E. Oppenheim, "Rational Decisions and Intrinsic Valuations," *Ibid.*, p. 220. Dror, *Public Policymaking*, p. 166. Carl J. Friedrich, "On Rereading Machiavelli and Althusius: Reason, Rationality, and Religion," *Ibid., Nomos VII*, p. 179. See also Philip Green, *Deadly Logic. The Theory of Nuclear Deterrence*, Columbus, OH: Ohio State University Press, 1966, p. 191, who points out the difficulty in even finding a "national value set."

22. Lord Vansittart, *The Mist Procession*, London: Gollancz, 1958, pp. 468-469 and 536. Frankel, p. 164.

23. Isaiah Berlin, *Historical Inevitability*, London: Oxford University Press, 1955, pp. 76-77. Green, p. 224. Frankel, p. 163. Berlin concludes that there have to be some values, however general and however few, "that enter into the normal definition of what constitutes a sane human being" and that absent these values or ends, beings "can scarcely be described as human; still less as rational." Thus, in extreme cases, "pursuit, or failure to pursue, certain ends can be regarded as evidence of—and in extreme cases part of the definition of—irrationality." Isaiah Berlin, "Rationality of Value Judgments," *Nomos VII*, p. 223.

24. Dror, *Crazy States*, p. 23; Booth, p. 69.

25. O.R. Holsti cited in Margaret G. Hermann, "Effects of Personal Characteristics of Political Leaders on Foreign Policy," *Why Nations Act. Theoretical Perspectives for Comparative Foreign Policy Studies*, eds., Maurice A. East, Stephen A. Salmore, Charles F. Hermann, London: Sage Publishers, 1978, p. 50.

26. G.D. Paige, *Political Leadership*, New York: The Free Press, 1972, p. 69.

27. Norman Rich, *Hitler's War Aims*, Vol. I, New York: Norton, 1973, p. 11. Klaus Hildebrand, *The Foreign Policy of the Third Reich*, trans. Anthony Fathergill, Berkeley: University of California Press, 1973, and

Andreas Hillgruber, *Hitlers Strategie. Politik und Kriegsführung 1940-1,* Frankfurt: Bernard and Graefe, 1965. See also Ian Kershaw, *The Nazi Dictatorship. Problems and Perspectives of Interpretation,* London: Edw. Arnold Ltd., 1985, pp. 61-62.

28. Joachim C. Fest, *The Face of the Third Reich. Portraits of the Nazi Leadership,* New York: Pantheon Books, 1970, p. 302. The earlier works were: Ernst Fraenkel, *The Dual State,* New York: Oxford University Press, 1942, and Franz Neumann, *Behemoth. The Structure and Practice of National Socialism,* London: Oxford University Press, 1942. See also Kershaw, p. 65.

29. Hans Mommsen, *Beamtentum im Dritten Reich,* Stuttgart: DVA, 1966; Peter Diehl-Thiele, *Partie und Staat im Dritten Reich,* Munich: C.H. Beck, 1969; Peter Hüttenberger, *Die Gauleiter. Studie zum Wandel des Machtgefüges in der NSDAP,* Stuttgart: DVA, 1969, and Edward N. Petersen, *The Limits of Hitler's Power,* Princeton: Princeton University Press, 1969. See also Kershaw, p. 66.

30. O.R. Holsti, "The Belief System and National Images: A Case Study," *Journal of Conflict Resolution,* No. 6, 1962, p. 244.

31. Alexander L. George, "The 'Operational Code'. A Neglected Approach to the Study of Political Leaders and Decision-Making," *International Studies Quarterly,* Vol. 13, No. 2, June 1969, p. 197. The concept of the operational code was first developed by N. Lertes, *The Operational Code of the Politburo,* New York: McGraw-Hill, 1951. For other works that follow the George construct, see O.R. Holsti, "The 'Operational Code' Approach to the Study of Political Leaders: John Foster Dulles, Philosophical and Instrumental Beliefs," *Canadian Journal of Political Science,* No. 3, 1970, pp. 123-157, and B. Thordarson, *Trudeau and Foreign Policy: A Study in Decision Making,* Toronto: Oxford University Press, 1972.

32. George, p. 221. See also *Ibid.,* pp. 201-217.

33. *Ibid.,* p. 200.

34. George, pp. 195 and 197. See also Alfred L. Rowse, *Appeasement,* New York: Norton, 1961, pp. 116-117, who pointed out in respect to British statesmen:

Not one of these men in high place [sic] in those years ever so much as read *Mein Kampf,* or would listen to anybody who had. They really did not know what they were dealing with, or the nature and degree of the evil thing they were up against. To be so uninstructed—a condition that arose in part from a certain

85

superciliousness, a lofty smugness, as well as superficiality of mind—was in itself a kind of dereliction of duty.

35. Walter C. Langer, *The Mind of Adolf Hitler. The Secret Wartime Report,* New York: Basic Books, 1972, p. 74.

36. Frankel, p. 115. One example of motivation could be emotional insecurity or low self-esteem on the part of the leader who then compensates with a drive for power. Harold Lasswell, *Power and Personality,* New York: Norton, 1948. In this construct, the greater this need for power by the national policymaker, the more forceful and aggressive his nation's foreign policy will be. D.G. Winter, *The Power Motive,* New York: The Free Press, 1973.

37. Langer, p. 126. "Probably none of us is entirely 'normal'," Hitler noted in 1941. *Adolf Hitler, Hitler's Secret Conversations, 1941-1944,* trans. Normal Cameron and R.H. Stevens, New York: Farrar, Straus, and Young, 1953, December 28-29, 1941, p. 127. William Carr, "The Hitler Image in the Last Half-Century," H.W. Koch ed., *Aspects of the Third Reich,* London: Macmillan, 1985. Examples of Hitler psycho-histories: Rudolf Binion, *Hitler Among the Germans,* New York: Elsevier, 1976, and Robert Waite, *Adolf Hitler. The Psychopathic God,* New York: Basic Books, 1977. In terms of Hitler, one historian has noted that even

if the finds were less dependent on conjecture and speculation, it is difficult to see how this approach could help greatly in explaining how such a person could become ruler of Germany and how his ideological paranoia came to be implemented as government policy by nonparanoids and nonpsychopaths in a sophisticated bureaucratic system.

Kershaw, p. 63. Another critic has inquired sarcastically, in this regard:

Does our understanding of National Socialist politics really depend on whether Hitler had only one testicle?...Perhaps the Fuehrer had three, which made things difficult for him—who knows?...Even if Hitler could be regarded irrefutably as a sadomasochist, which scientific interest does that further?...Does the 'final solution of the Jewish question' thus become more easily understandable or the "twisted road to Auschwitz" become the one-way street of a psychopath in power?

Hans-Ulrich Wehler, "Psychoanalysis and History," *Social Research.* No. 47, 1980, p. 531.

38. Booth, p. 13.

39. *Ibid.*, p. 20. The problem of projecting assumptions about rational behavior is compounded when organizational models and governmental politics are added to the unitary actor model. Bureaucracies, for instance, have their own cultural idiosyncratic characteristics, and there is always the danger of projecting one norm of bureaucratic behavior onto those of another nation. *Ibid.*, p. 65.

40. *Ibid.*, p. 94. On "unrealistic, exaggerated diabolism," see Ralph K. White, *Nobody Wanted War: Misperceptions in Vietnam and Other Wars*, Garden City, NY: Doubleday, 1968, p. 318. See also Alix Strachey, *The Unconscious Motives of War*, New York: International Universities Press, 1957, pp. 202-203.

41. Booth, p. 95. "In general the art of all truly great national leaders at all times consists among other things primarily in not dividing the attention of a people, but in concentrating it upon a single foe." Adolf Hitler, *Mein Kampf*, trans. Ralph Manheim, Boston: Houghton Mifflin, 1943, p. 118.

42. Rauschning, p. 137.

43. Chester Wilmot, *The Struggle for Europe*, London: Collins, 1952, p. 21. Booth, pp. 85-86. Fred C. Ikle, *How Nations Negotiate*, New York: Harper & Row, 1964, pp. 82 and 104.

44. Booth, p. 60. Robert Jervis, *Perceptions and Misperceptions in International Politics*, Princeton: Princeton University Press, 1976, p. 193, and *The Logic of Images in International Relations*, Princeton: Princeton University Press, 1970, p. 205. Hans J. Morgenthau, *Politics Among Nations. The Struggle for Power and Peace*, New York: Alfred A. Knopf, 1967, p. 63.

45. Alan Bullock, *Hitler. A Study in Tyranny*, New York: Harper & Row, 1962, p. 528.

46. For a similar model, see David Braybrooke and Charles E. Lindblom, *A Strategy of Decision. Policy Evaluation as a Social Process*, London: Free Press of Glencoe, 1963, p. 67. "Most of the actions taken by bureaucracies involve doing again or continuing to do what was done in the past. In the absence of some reason to change their behavior, organizations keep doing what they have been doing." M.H. Halperin, *Bureaucratic Politics and Foreign Policy*, Washington, DC: The Brookings Institution, 1974, p. 99.

47. Gordon A. Craig, "The German Foreign Office from Neurath to Ribbentrop," *The Diplomats. Vol. 2. The Thirties*, eds. Gordon A. Craig and Felix Gilbert, New York: Antheneum, 1963, p. 410.

48. *Ibid.*, p. 413.

49. Braybrooke and Lindblom, p. 68.

50. Albert Speer, *Inside the Third Reich,* trans. Richard and Clara Winston, New York: Macmillan, 1970, p. 169.

51. Ole R. Holsti, *Crisis Escalation War,* Montreal: McGill-Queen's University Press, 1972, p. 208. Booth, p. 116. See also Leon Festinger, *A Theory of Cognitive Dissonance,* Stanford: Stanford University Press, 1957. "As long as Prussia limited herself to purely European foreign policy aspirations," Hitler wrote as early as 1928, "she had no serious danger to fear from England." Adolf Hitler, *Hitler's Secret Book,* trans. Salvator Attanasio, New York: Bramhill House, 1986, p. 151.

52. Bullock, p. 550. See also D.C. Watt, "The Debate Over Hitler's Foreign Policy—Problems of Reality or Faux Problemes?" *Deutsche Frage und europaisches Gleichgewicht,* eds. Klaus Hildebrand and Reiner Pommerin, Cologne: Boehlau, 1985, p. 165.

53. *Secret Conversations,* August 4, 1942, p. 496. See also *Ibid.,* February 9, 1942, p. 249; Bullock, pp. 771-772, and Reynolds, p. 126. See also Martin van Creveld, "War Lord Hitler: Some Points Reconsidered," *European Studies Review,* January 1974, p. 75, who points out that "one should keep in mind that Hitler never intended to fight a World War in the first place." As late as August 31, 1944, Hitler still could not get over British actions in 1939 as well as the British refusal to compromise after the German victories in the West in 1940. "I have proved that I did everything to come to some understanding with the English," he concluded. Felix Gilbert, ed., *Hitler Directs His War,* New York: Octagon Books, 1982, p. 105.

54. *Secret Conversations,* September 25, 1941, p. 35.

55. Heinz Guderian, *Panzer Leader,* trans. Constantine Fitzgibbon, New York: E.P. Dutton, 1952, p. 407; Bullock, p. 775.

56. There is a natural tendency to see decision makers who lose as unreasonably tied to their views, disregarding correct information. But in most cases, those judged by history to have been right have demonstrated no more openness to new information nor willingness to modify their images than those like Hitler who were wrong. For example, the anti-appeasement policy of Robert Vansittart, the Permanent Undersecretary in the British Foreign Office, has generally been viewed as an example of foresight and courage. In fact, like Chamberlain, he fitted each bit of information about the Nazi regime, no matter how ambiguous, into his own hypothesis without an openminded analysis to see if the explanations proffered by the appeasers accounted better for the information than did his own preconceptions. It is often forgotten, in this regard, that Hitler in the 1930s was the exception that made the anti-appeaser's case. Under conservative

leaders, Germany would not have run a high risk in order to regain a powerful European position and thus would have been appeased. "Had Hitler not come to power," Robert Jervis has pointed out, "many of the Englishmen who now seem wise would have been dangerous warmongers." p. 25. Jervis, *Perception,* p. 180. See also *Ibid.,* pp. 119-120, 128-130, 138, 151-153, 172, and 176; Verba, pp. 94-95; Ian Colvin, *Vansittart in Office,* London: Golancz, 1965, p. 23; and Martin Gilbert and Richard Gott, *The Appeasers,* London: Weidenfield and Nicolson, 1963, p. 34.

57. Walter Schellenberg, *The Schellenberg Memoirs,* ed. and trans. Louis Hagen, London: Andre Deutich, 1956, p. 209. Betts, p. 133.

58. Barton Whaley, *Codeword BARBAROSSA,* Cambridge: The MIT Press, 1973, pp. 14-15, 50 and 251. See also Eberhard Jäckel, *Hitler's Weltanschaung. A Blueprint for Power,* Middletown, CT: Wesleyan University Press, 1972, p. 45, and Wolfgang Michalka, "From the Anti-Comintern Pact to the Euro-Asiatic Bloc: Ribbentrop's Alternative Concept of Hitler's Foreign Policy Programme," in Koch, p. 283, who points out that pivotal role of Hitler's perception of Britain's irrational stubborness: Hitler was only able to explain the decision of the British government to continue the war despite its hopeless position and not to act upon his suggestions of an alliance by thinking that London was still counting on two allies, the United States and the Soviet Union, so that in time an enormous anti-Hitler coalition could be formed, aimed at gradually starving out and finally conquering the German Reich, in much the same way as in the last phase of the First World War.

59. Alan Clark, *Barbarossa: The Russo-German Conflict, 1941-45,* New York: Morrow, 1965, p. 23. Betts, pp. 133ff. Schellenberg, p. 208. Wilhelm Keitel, *The Memoirs of Field Marshal Keitel,* ed. Walter Gorlitz, trans. David Irving, New York: Stein and Day, 1966, p. 122.

60. Martin van Creveld, *Supplying War: Logistics from Wallenstein to Patton,* Cambridge: Cambridge University Press, 1977, pp. 150-151 and 154.

61. Dror, *Crazy States,* p. 60. R.C. Snyder and J.A. Robinson, *National and International Decision-Making,* New York: The Institute for International Order, 1961, p. 164. Margaret G. Hermann, "Effects of Personal Characteristics," p. 60.

62. Raushning, p. 280.

63. *Ibid.,* p. 81.

64. *Ibid.,* pp. 277, 280-281.

65. *Mein Kampf*, pp. 516, 660; Raushning, p. 134.

66. Kurt Ludecke, *I Knew Hitler*, London: Unwin, 1938, pp. 217ff. Joachim Fest, "On Remembering Adolf Hitler," *Encounter*, Vol. XLI, No. 4, October 1973, p. 30. "I shall attain my purpose without a struggle, by legal means...." Rauschning, p. 107. "When I was younger," Hitler declared in 1941, "I thought it was necessary to set about matters with dynamite. I've since realized that there's room for a little subtlety." *Secret Conversations*, December 13, 1941, p. 117.

67. Fest, "On Remembering," p. 31, and *Faces*, p. 41.

68. Handel, pp. 31-32.

69. *Secret Conversations*, November 2, 1941, p. 88. "The basic notions that served us in the struggle for power have proved that they are correct, and are the same notions as we apply today in the struggle we are waging on a world scale." *Ibid.*, November 19, 1941, p. 110.

70. John Thomas Emmerson, *The Rhineland Crisis*, Ames, IA: Iowa University Press, 1977, p. 101. Handel, p. 52.

71. Rauschning, p. 11. See also *Ibid.*, pp. 109-110:

I am willing to sign anything. I will do anything to facilitate the success of my policy. I am prepared to guarantee all frontiers and to make non-aggression pacts and friendly alliances with anybody. It would be sheer stupidity to refuse to make use of such measures merely because one might possibly be driven into a position where a solemn promise would have to be broken. There has never been a sworn treaty which has not sooner or later been broken or become untenable. There is no such thing as an everlasting treaty. Anyone whose conscience is so tender that he will not sign a treaty unless he can feel sure he can keep it in all and any circumstances is a fool. Why should one not please others and facilitate matters for oneself by signing pacts if the others believe that something is thereby accomplished or regulated? Why should I not make an agreement in good faith today and unhesitatingly break it tomorrow if the future of the German people demands it?

72. Emmerson, p. 291. Handel. p. 58.

73. Handel, pp. 58. 60-61.

74. Fest. *Face*. p. 183.

75. Herbert Feis, *The Road to Pearl Harbor*, Princeton: Princeton University Press, 1950, p. 202. Jervis, *Logic*, p. 106.

76. Frankel, p. 172. Jervis, *Perception,* p. 278. "When I first met him," the British ambassador remarked of Hitler, "his logic and sense of realities had impressed me, but as time went on he appeared to me to become more and more... convinced of his own infallibility and greatness...." Sir Nevile Henderson, *Failure of a Mission,* New York: Putnam's, 1940, p.177.

77. Frankel, p. 172. Fest, *Face,* pp. 39 and 50, and "On Remembering," p. 31. "I couldn't say whether my feeling that I am indispensable has been strengthened during this war. One thing is certain, that without me the decisions to which we today owe our existence would not have been taken." *Secret Conversations,* October 13-14, 1941, p. 48.

78. Karl Dietrich Bracher, *Adolf Hitler,* Berne/Munich/ Vienna: Droste, 1964, p. 12. Fest, "On Remembering," p. 26.

79. Fest, *Face,* p. 44.

80. *Secret Conversations,* February 26-27, 1942, p. 276.

81. Fest, *Face,* p. 83.

82. Jeremy Noakes and Geoffrey Pridham, *Documents on Nazism,* London: Unwin, 1974, p. 256. Kershaw, pp. 74-75.

83. Noakes and Pridham, p. 261. Kershaw, p. 75. Fest, *Face,* pp. 127-128 and 131. "What would happen to me if I didn't have around me men whom I completely trust, to do the work for which I can't find time?" *Secret Conversations,* October 13-14, 1941, p. 48.

84. Koch, pp. 184-185.

85. Noakes and Pridham, p. 245. Joseph Nyomarkay, *Charisma and Factionalism Within the Nazi Party*, Minneapolis: University of Minnesota Press, 1967, pp. 70-71. "The best organization is not that which inserts the greatest, but that which inserts the smallest, intermediary apparatus between the leadership of a movement and its individual adherents." *Mein Kampf*, p. 346.

86. "I am often urged to say something in praise of bureaucracy—I can't do it." *Secret Conversations,* August 1-2, 1941, p. 15. See also *Ibid.,* August 26, 1942, p. 336. "In olden times it was the strolling player who was buried in the public refuse-heap; today it is the lawyer who should be buried there. No one stands closer in mentality to the criminal than the lawyer...." *Ibid.,* July 22, 1942, p. 475.

91

87. Hugh R. Trevor-Roper, *The Last Days of Hitler*, London: The Macmillan Company, 1947, p. 202.

88. Kershaw, p. 73. On the feudal aspects, see Robert Koehl, "Future Aspects of National Socialism," Henry A. Turner, ed., *Nazism and the Third Reich*, New York: Quadrangle Books, 1972, pp. 151-174. See also Hans Mommsen, "National Socialism: Continuity and Change," Walter Laquer, ed., *Fascism. A Reader's Guide*, 2nd ed., London: Penguin, 1979, pp. 176-178, and Jane Coplan, "Bureaucracy, Politics and the National Socialist State," Peter D. Stachura, ed., *The Shaping of the Nazi State*, London: Croom Helm, 1978, pp. 234-256.

89. John M. Collins, *Grand Strategy*, Annapolis, MD: Naval Institute Press, 1973, p. 277.

90. Dror, *Crazy States*, p. 17.

91. Jervis, *Perception*, p. 52.

92. Speer, p. 72. General von Blomberg pointed out after the war that if the French had resisted, the Germans would "have to have beat a hasty retreat." And Keitel confided that "he wouldn't have been a bit surprised" if three battalions of French troops had flicked the German forces right off the map. G.M. Gilbert, *The Psychology of Dictatorship*, New York: Ronald Press, 1950, p. 211. But see also Emmerson, p. 105, who concludes that the "French army of 1936 had no strike force capable of marching as far as Mainz, to say nothing of occupying the whole of the demilitarized zone. Nor did it possess a single unit which could be made instantly combat ready."

93. "In the past the French produced a Talleyrand and a Fouche; today they have become humdrum and circumspect, a nation of dried-up clerks. They will venture to play for halfpence, but no longer for a great stake." Rauschning, p. 277. For additional measures Hitler took to lower the risk by keeping the operation as unprovocative as possible, see Emmerson, p. 97 and Handel, p. 61.

94. This did not mean, of course, that Hitler was not nervous. "The forty-eight hours after the march," he stated, "....were the most nerve-wracking in my life." Bullock, p. 345. But see *Secret Conversations*, January 27, 1942 and May 21, 1942, pp. 211-212 and 406-407.

95. Jervis, *Logic*, p. 205 and *Perception*, p. 52.

96. Original emphasis. Franz Halder, *The Halder Diaries. The Private War Journals of Colonel General Franz Halder*, ed. Arnold Lissance, Boulder, CO, and Dunn Loring, VA: Westview Press and T.N. Dupuy Associates, 1976, Volume I, p. 8.

97. A.J.P. Taylor, "War Origins Again," *The Origins of the Second World War*, ed. Esmonde Robertson, London: Macmillan, 1971, p. 139.

98. Jervis, *Perception*, p. 53.

99. *Secret Conversations*, January 5-6, 1942, p. 150.

100. *Ibid.*, October 17-18, 1941, p. 58.

101. Betts, p. 130.

102. *Ibid.*, p. 145. Telford Taylor, *The March of Conquest. The German Victories in Western Europe*, 1940, New York: Simon & Schuster, 1958, p. 158.

103. *Secret Conversations*, January 5-6, 1942, p. 150.

104. *Ibid.*, August 26, 1942, p. 537. "The more we see of conditions in Russia, the more thankful we must be that we struck in time." *Ibid.*, July 22, 1942, p. 476. "If to-day you do harm to the Russians, it is so as to avoid giving them the opportunity of doing harm to us. *Ibid.*, September 23, 1941, p. 35.

105. David Irving, *Hitler's War*, New York: Viking Press, 1977, p. 180. See also H.W. Koch, "Hitler's Programme and the Genesis of Operation Barbarossa," in Koch, pp. 319-320, Betts, pp. 143-144, and Watt, p. 163.

106. Betts, pp. 137-138 and 144.

107. *Ibid.*, p. 144. See also Samuel P. Huntington, *The Common Defense*, New York: Columbia University Press, 1961, p.206, who noted that "risks cannot be calculated, they can only be felt."

108. *Fuehrer Conferences on Naval Affairs 1939-1945*, London: Greenhill Books, 1990, pp. 119 and 136.

109. *Secret Conversations*, October 13, 1941, p. 46.

110. Bullock, p. 754.

111. For a similar diagram and description, see Dror, *Public Policymaking*, pp. 149, 151-152. See also Annatol Rapoport and A.M. Gharmmah, *Prisoner's Dilemma*, Ann Arbor: University of Michigan, 1965.

112. Eugene E. Jennings, *An Anatomy of Leadership*, New York: Harper & Brothers, 1960, p. 98. Dror, *Public Policymakers*, p. 158.

113. Rauschning, p. 6.

114. Langer, pp. 33 and 159. *Mein Kampf*, p. 29.

115. Original emphasis. Rauschning, p. 181.

116. *Ibid.*, p. 181.

117. *Ibid.*

118. Langer, p. 29. Bullock, p. 378.

119. *Secret Conversations*, September 17, 1941, p. 26. Jennings, pp. 73-74. "Only the man who acts becomes conscious of the real world." Rauschning, p. 224.

120. Fest, *Face*, p. 187.

121. Fest, "On Remembering," p. 24.

122. *Ibid.*, p. 25. *Mein Kampf*, pp. 234 and 459. Fest, *Face*, p. 300. See H.A. Trevor - Roper, "The Mind of Hitler," *Secret Conversations*, pp. xxv-xxvi, who points out that "Hitler was more practical than his own doctrinaire followers," believing "the general truth of the doctrine," but lacking any "patience with the theological niceties" of such priests as Himmler and Rosenberg. Rosenberg never realized that the ideology he believed in so fervently carried no weight in the centers of power, as shown by Hitler's musings during the war:

> I must insist that Rosenberg's 'The Myth of theTwentieth Century' is not to be regarded as an expression of the official doctrine of the Party. The moment the book appeared, I deliberately refrained from recognising [sic] it as any such thing....It is interesting to note that comparatively few of the older members of the Party are to be found among the readers of Rosenberg's book, and that the publishers had, in fact, great difficulty in disposing of the first edition....It gives me considerable pleasure to realise [sic] that the book has been closely studied only by our opponents. Like most of the Gauleiters, I have myself merely glanced cursorily at it. It is in any case written in much too abstruse a style, in my opinion.

Ibid., April 11, 1942, p. 342.

123. Weber, Essays in Sociology, pp. 116-117. Hilsman, pp. 66-67.

124. One manifestation of this trend was grotesquely illustrated long before the *Machtübernahme* by death notices in which Hitler replaced God. And after 1933, there was the prayer used in Nazi day care centers that ended: "Füehrer, my Füehrer, my faith, my light." Fest, *Face*, pp. 41, 188, 367. Nevertheless, there was more than just a simplistic deistic connection

between the Führer and the Gefuhrten. For it was chiefly in an "inner" sense, as Karl Dietrich Bracher has pointed out,

> that Hitler was presented as the revealer of a new meaning to life, one which absorbed his followers' needs to surrender themselves, to serve him and to submit to him, to shed their weariness of responsibility, and as one who alone was capable of translating this need into the release of political action. He was the incarnation of the 'people's community'; thanks to his intuition and leadership talent he was always right, he was the unchallengeable interpreter of their interests. For this reason he was not subject, even vis-a-vis his own followers, to any rules of law.

Karl Dietrich Bracher, *The Age of Ideologies, A History of Political Thought in the Twentieth Century*, New York: St. Martin's, 1984, p. 122.

125. Fest, *Face*, p. 46.

126. *Ibid.*, p. 49. See also Dorothy Thompson's description quoted in Langer, p. 57.

> At Garmisch I met an American from Chicago. He had been at Oberammergau, at the Passion Play. "These people are all crazy," he said. "This is not a revolution, it's a revival. They think Hitler is God. Believe it or not, a German woman sat next to me at the Passion Play and when they hoisted Jesus on the Cross, she said, 'There he is. That is our Füehrer, our Hitler.' And when they paid out the thirty pieces of silver to Judas, she said: 'That is Roehm, who betrayed the Leader.'

127. *Secret Conversations*, August 20, 1942, p. 524.

128. Kershaw, p. 76. Petersen, p. 7. See also Lothar Kettenacker, "Social and Psychological Aspects of the Führer's Rule," in Koch, pp. 101-102, who emphasizes the link between charismatic rule and the internal chaos of the Third Reich. It was Hitler's role of "overlord" of the underbureaucratic, almost neo-feudalistic system of government that "appealed to some atavistic instincts of a still strongly dynastic oriented society."

129. Herman Kahn, *On Escalation*, New York: Praeger, 1965, p. 57. Reynolds, p. 106.

130. Thomas Schelling, *Arms and Influence*, New Haven: Yale University Press, 1966, p. 37 and *The Strategy of Conflict*, Cambridge: Harvard University Press, 1960, p. 17. See, however, Green, p. 164, who was obviously not considering the concept of crazy states when he noted

of Schelling's examples that "one can only say that anything is possible but that ordinarily we hope for a little more assurance about the way the arts of statesmanship are being practiced than we would find in an institution for the mentally ill."

131. *Mein Kampf*, p. 18.

132. Bullock, p. 528. By this time, Sir Nevile Henderson, the British Ambassador, believed Hitler was a psychopath, given to extreme and sudden fits of rage and often influenced by sudden bursts of intuition. Felix Gilbert, "Two British Ambassadors: Perth and Henderon," *The Diplomats*, p. 543. On Hitler's reputation with his subordinates as a Teppichfresser, see William L. Shirer, *Berlin Diary*, New York: Knopf, 1941, p. 137. All of Hitler's anger, of course, was not just pure calculation. In 1938, for instance, Hitler built up an extraordinary rage against Czechoslovakia, marked not only by the violence of his language, but even of his internal communications. Watt, p. 164.

133. Dror, *Crazy States*, pp. 23-24.

134. Hillgruber, Jäckel, and Hildebrand. As an example, Jäckel states that by the completion of his 1928 unpublished second book, Hitler's conception of foreign policy, although "still riddied with contradictions and absurdities," was complete. It was a concept already demonstrating "a high degree of purposeful orientation, consistency, and coherence. Here we have clearly defined political goals and an indication of the means which might be used to strive for and possibly attain these goals." Jäckel, pp. 40 and 42. Kershaw, pp. 63-64 and 108.

135. Karl Dietrich Bracher, "The Stages of Totalitarian Integration (Gleichschaltung)," in Hajo Holborn, ed., *Republic to Reich. The Making of the Nazi Revolution*, New York: Praeger, 1973, p. 128 and *The German Dictatorship*, trans. Jean Steinberg, New York: Praeger, 1970, pp. 247-259.

136. Martin Broszat, *The Hitler State*, London: 1981, p. 9, and "Soziale Motivation und Führer-Bindung des Nationalsozialismus," *Vierteljahrshefte für Zeitgeschichte*, 18 (1970), pp. 407-409. Kershaw, pp. 67 and 110-111.

137. *Ibid.*, p. 85. Lucy Dawidowicz, *The War Against the Jews. 1933-1945*, New York: Harmondsworth, 1975, pp. 198-208.

138. Martin Broszat, "The Genesis of the 'Final Solution'," in Koch, p. 405. Hans Mommsen, "National Socialism: Continuity and Change," p. 179. Kershaw, p. 87.

139. *Secret Conversations*, May 12, 1942, p. 380. Kettenacker, pp. 129-130.

140. Kershaw, p. 100. For the speech, see Jäckel, p. 61. But see also Koch, p. 459.

141. Kershaw, p. 105.

142. *Ibid.*, p. 104.

143. For the basic concept, see Dror. *Crazy States*, p. 43.

144. *Ibid.*, pp. 39-45.

145. On the primacy of political decades over economics, see Tim Mason, "The Primacy of Politics—Politics and Economics in National Socialist Germany," in Turner, p. 175, who concludes "that both the domestic and foreign policy of the National Socialist government became, from 1936 onward, increasingly independent of the influence of the economic ruling classes, and even in some essential aspects ran contrary to their collective interests." For similar opinions, see Kershaw, p. 51, and Richard J. Overy, *The Nazi Economic Recovery 1932-1938*. London: Oxford University Press, 1982, p. 58. But see William Carr, *Arms. Autarky and Aggression*, 3nd ed., London: Oxford University Press, 1979. p. 65. who points out that "Ideological, strategic and economic factors are too closely intermeshed in a country's foreign policy to permit a clinical separation."

146. Burton H. Klein, *Germany's Economic Preparation for War*. Cambridge, MA: Harvard University Press, 1959. pp. 76-82.

147. Raushning, p. 20. "Even to Schacht, I had to begin by explaining this elementary truth: that the essential cause of the stability of our currency was to be sought for in our concentration camps. The currency remains stable when the speculators are put under lock and key." *Secret Conversations*, October 15, 1941, p. 54. Klein, pp. 76-82.

148. *Ibid.*, p. 46, and Koch, "Introduction to Part III," in Koch. pp. 328-329.

149. *Ibid.* Tim Mason, "The Legacy of 1918 for National Socialism," in Anthony Nicholls and Erich Matthias, eds., *German Democracy and the Triumph of Hitler. Essays in Recent German History*, London: George Allen & Unwin, Ltd., 1971, p. 231.

150. *Mein Kampf*, p. 192.

151. *Secret Book*, pp. 95-96. "Foreign policy must secure the life of a people for its domestic political development. *Ibid.*, p. 34. "The impossibility of justifying the necessity for enduring the war helped to bring about its unfortunate outcome." *Ibid.*, p. 77.

152. Raushning, pp. 212-213. Fest, *Face,* p. 43. Mason, "Legacy," p 230.

153. *Secret Conversations,* July 28, 1942, p. 487. Karl Hardach, *The Political Economy of Germany in the Twentieth Century,* Berkeley, 1980, pp. 76-79. Kershaw, p. 78. "The Füehrer understands the Navy's difficulties....He explains in detail how he must first of all prevent a collapse of any front where the enemy could substantially injure home territory." *Füehrer Conferences,* December 22, 1942, p. 304.

154. Speer, p. 214. Mason, "Legacy," pp. 226-227 and 239.

155. Jäckel, p. 67.

156. Karl Manheim, *Man and Society in an Age of Reconstruction,* New York. Paterson, 1940, pp. 49-75. Green, pp. 216-217 and 315.

157. Mason, "Primacy," p. 195. Brosgart, "Genesis," pp. 409-410. Kershaw, pp. 57-58.

158. Bernd Wegner, "The 'Aristocracy of National Socialism': The Role of the SS in National Socialist Germany," in Koch, p. 444.

159. David Irving, *The Mare's Nest,* Boston: Little, Brown & Company, 1964, p. 304. See also Peter G. Cooksley, *Flying Bomb: The Story of Hitler's V Weapons in World War II,* New York: Charles Scribner's Sons, 1979, and Basil Collier, *The Battle for the V-Weapons 1944-1945,* New York: Morrow, 1965. The code name for the SAM was 'Waterfall': Speer, pp. 364-365. The Me-262 fighter plane, with two jet engines and a speed of over 500 miles per hour, was the most valuable of the German 'secret weapons'. In September 1943, however, without explanation, Hitler ordered preparations for large-scale production of the jet to stop. In January 1944, he ordered resumption of production, but directed that the plane, which was built to be a fighter, was to be used as a fast bomber. Despite objections, Hitler, not surprisingly, prevailed. But the element of useful surprise had been lost through this change in role and the concomitant production delays. *Ibid.,* pp.362-363.

160. David Irving, *The German Atomic Bomb. The History of Nuclear Research in Nazi Germany,* New York: Simon and Shuster, 1967, pp. 231 and 299. Green, p. 187. For similar problems in Britain concerning intragovernmental disputes over radar and strategic bombing, see C.P. Snow, *Science and Government,* Cambridge: Harvard University Press, 1961.

161. Until the chemical industry was bombed in 1944, German production amounted to 3100 tons of mustard gas and 1000 tons of Tabun per month. Speer, p. 413. See also Stephen L. McFarland, "Preparing for

What Never Came: Chemical and Biological Warfare in World War II,"
Defense Analysis, Volume 2, June 1986, p. 113 and John Ellis van Courland
Moon, "Chemical Weapons and Deterrence: The World War II Experience,"
International Security, Volume 8, No. 4, Spring 1984, p. 25.

162. *Mein Kampf,* pp. 201-202. See also *Ibid.,* p. 279, for the seeds
of later policy in this experience.

> If at the beginning of the War and during the War twelve or fifteen
> thousand of these Hebrew corrupters of the people had been held
> under poison gas, as happened to hundreds of thousands of our
> very best German workers in the field, the sacrifice of millions at
> the front would not have been in vain. On the contrary: twelve
> thousand scoundrels eliminated in time might have saved the lives
> of a million real Germans, valuable for the future.

163. But in conversations during the early 1930s, Hitler pointed out that
a "nation denied its rights may use any weapon, even bacterial warfare. I
have no scruples, and I will use whatever weapon I require. The new poison
gases are horrible. But there is no difference between a slow death in
barbed-wire entanglements and the agonized death of a gassed man or
one poisoned by bacteria." Raushning, pp. 3-4.

164. Speer, pp. 413-414 and McFarland, p. 114. "Anyone," the
German Army Chief of Gas Operations testified after the war, "who
suggested in Germany that chemical warfare should be initiated would have
been called 'an idiot' and 'crazy.'" *Ibid.,* p. 113. Green, pp. 208-209.

165. Irving, *German Atomic Bomb,* p. 241.

166. *Ibid.,* pp. 241-242. "I am sure that Hitler would not have hesitated
for a moment to employ atom bombs against England." Speer, p. 227.

167. *Ibid.,* p. 228.

168. Irving, *German Atomic Bomb,* p. 255.

169. *Ibid.,* p. 295.

170. *Ibid.* One result was that Speer consistently underestimated
Germany's nuclear effort. "At best," he wrote, "with extreme concentration
of all our resources, we could have had a German atom bomb by 1947...."
Speer, p. 229.

171. Irving, *German Atomic Bomb,* p. 233. "When one considers that
right up to the end of the war in 1945," the deputy director of the German
project recalled, "there was virtually no increase in our heavy water stocks
in Germany, and that for the last experiments in 1945 there was in fact only

two and a half tons of heavy water available, it will be seen that it was the elimination of German heavy water production in Norway that was the main factor in our failure to achieve a self-sustaining atomic reactor before the war ended." *Ibid.*, p. 211.

172. *Secret Conversations*, December 28-29, 1941, p. 127.

173. Trevor-Roper, "Mind of Hitler," p. xxiii.

174. Efraim Karsh, "In Baghdad, Politics is a Lethal Game," *The New York Times Magazine*, September 30, 1990, p. 42. George Lardner, Jr., "Saddam's Inner Circle Seen as Unquestioning," *The Washington Post*, December 3, 1990, p. A1.

175. Patrick E. Tyler, "Saddam, in Grasping, Tends to Overreach," *The Washington Post*. August 7, 1990, p. A9.

176. Karsh, p. 39.

177. Roger Parkinson, *Peace for Our Time. Munich to Dunkirk—The Inside Story*, New York: McKay, 1971, p. 103. Kenneth Boulding, "National Images and International Systems," *Journal of Conflict Resolution*, June 3. 1959, p. 127. Jervis, *Perception*, pp. 82-83. Betts, p. 142. A self-fulfilling prophecy is "a false definition of the situation which makes the originally false conception come true." Robert Merton, *Social Theory and Social Structure*. Glencoe, IL: Free Press, 1957, p. 423.

178. Jervis, *Perceptions*, p. 85.

179. N.L. Bukharin, *Imperialism and World Economy*, New York: H. Fertig, 1929, p. 114.

180. Morganthau, p. 59. The problem in assessing motivation is summed up in Glen Snyder and Paul Diesing, *Conflict Among Nations. Bargaining, Decision Making, and System Structure in International Crises*. Princeton: Princeton University Press, 1977, p. 254:

> Whether to be firm and tough toward an adversary, in order to deter him, but at the risk of provoking his anger or fear and heightened conflict, or to conciliate him in the hope of reducing sources of conflict, but at the risk of strengthening him and causing him to miscalculate one's own resolve, is a perennial and central dilemma of international relations. A rational resolution of this dilemma depends most of all on an accurate assessment of the long run interests and intentions of the opponent. If his aims are limited, conciliation of his specific grievances may be cheaper than engaging in a power struggle

with him. If they are possibly unlimited, the rational choice is to deter him with countervailing power and a resolve to use it.

181. Rauschning, p. 118. Morganthau, pp. 65-66.

182. Herman Kahn, *Thinking about the Unthinkable*. New York: Horizon Press, 1962, pp. 111-112. Dror, *Crazy States*, pp. 80-83. Schelling, *Strategy of Conflict*, pp. 11-13 and 197ff. Marion J. Levy, Jr., *The Structure of Society*. Princeton: Princeton University Press, 1952, pp. 242-246. Hitler, of course, understood the importance of credible deterrence. As early as 1928, he commented in his unpublished book on the capability of the "inner value" of the "iron fist" to "make its appearance so visibly...that merely the actuality of its existence must compell a regard for and an appraisal of this fact." *Secret Book.*, p. 124.

183. *On War*, p. 579.

184. Alexander M. Haig, Jr., "Gulf Analogy: Munich or Vietnam?", *The New York Times*, December 10, 1990, p. A-19.

185. Schelling, *Arms and Influence*, p. 86, and *Strategy of Conflict*, p. 20, the latter of which suggests the ancient institution of hostage taking may have to be reevaluated along with other devices, adding:

> We tend to identify peace, stability and the quiescence of conflict with notions like trust, good faith, and mutual respect. To the extent that this point of view actually encourages trust and respect it is good. But where trust and good faith do not exist and cannot be made to by our acting as though they did, we may wish to solicit advice from the underworld, or from ancient despotisms, on how to make agreements work when trust and good faith are lacking and there is no legal recourse for breach of contract. The ancients exchanged hostages, drank wine from the same glass to demonstrate the absence of poison, met in public places to inhibit the massacre of one by the other, and even deliberately exchanged spies to facilitate transmittal of authentic information. It seems likely that a well-developed theory of strategy could throw light on the efficacy of some of those old devices, suggest the circumstances to which they apply, and discover modern equivalents that, though offensive to our taste, may be desperately needed in the regulation of conflict.

186. *On War*, p. 125.

187. Georgie Anne Geyer, "Saddam has history of defeated heroes to build on," *Harrisburg Patriot*, December 5, 1990, p. A-13.

188. *Mein Kampf*, p. 229.

189. Trevor-Roper, *Last Days of Hitler*, p. 92. For Langer's prediction of Hitler's suicide, see Langer, p. 211.

190. Michael I. Handel, *War, Strategy and Intelligence*. London: Cass, 1989, p. 464.

191. Both August 31, 1944 quotes from Gilbert, *Hitler Directs His War*, pp. 105-106. See also *Ibid.*, pp. xxiv-xxv. The air of unreality, of course, grew stronger as the end drew near. Thus, there is the picture of Hitler's drawing encouragement from the news of President Roosevelt's death or through the rereading of Carlyle's work on Frederick the Great. Trevor-Roper, *Last Days*, pp. 112-113 and 214. How divorced from reality Hitler's minions could be was shown in Himmler's greeting to the representative of the World Jewish Congress who came to see him in April 1945: "Welcome to Germany, Herr Masur," the SS chief stated. "It is time you Jews and we National Sociatlists buried the hatchet." Fest, *Face*, p. 123.

192. Felix Gilbert noted that "in reading Hitler's case as it emerges from the records, it would appear that it is an oversimplification to view the contrasts between him and the Generals as one between professionals who act on the basis of rational considerations and a madman acting on the basis of intuition." Gilbert, *Hitler Directs His War*, p. xxiii. See also van Creveld, "War Lord Hitler," pp. 74-75. For a typical example of the military description of Hitler, see Guderian, pp. 414-415:

> His fists raised, his cheeks flushed with rage, his whole body trembling, the man stood there in front of me, beside himself with fury and having lost all self-control. After each outburst of rage Hitler would stride up and down the carpet-edge, then suddenly stop immediately before me and hurl his next accusation in my face. He was almost screaming, his eyes seemed about to pop out of his head and the veins stood out on his temples.

193. Francois Genoud, ed., *The Testament of Adolf Hitler: The Hitler-Bormann Documents*. February-April 1945, trans. R.H. Stevens. London: Cassell, 1961, p. 107.

194. Van Creveld, "War Lord Hitler," p. 79.

195. "By the year 2000," Secretary of Defense Cheney has pointed out in this regard,

more than two dozen developing nations will have ballistic missiles. 15 of those countries will have the scientific skills to make their own. and half of them either have or are near to getting nuclear capability. as well. Thirty countries will have chemical weapons and ten will be able to deploy biological weapons.

Secretary of Defense Dick Cheney. *Address to the Conservative Leadership Conference.* Washington. DC. November 9, 1990.

ABOUT THE AUTHOR

DAVID JABLONSKY is an Infantry Colonel in the U.S. Army. He has served throughout the United States, Vietnam and Europe (Federal Republic of Germany and Belgium). His most recent assignments were as Director of Military Strategy, Department of National Security and Strategy, U.S. Army War College; as a U.S. Army Chief of Staff Strategic Fellow; and in the Office of the Secretary of Defense. He holds a B.A. in European History from Dartmouth College; an M.A. in International Relations from Boston University; and an M.A. and Ph.D. in European History from the University of Kansas. He is currently Chairman, Strategic Research Department, Strategic Studies Institute, U.S. Army War College, and has held the Elihu Root Chair of Strategy. Colonel Jablonsky has written numerous articles and is the author of *The Nazi Party in Dissolution: Hitler and the Verbotzeit 1923-1925* (1989) and *Churchill, the Great Game and Total War* (1991).

U.S. ARMY WAR COLLEGE

Commandant
Major General Paul G. Cerjan

******

STRATEGIC STUDIES INSTITUTE

Director
Colonel Karl W. Robinson

Author
Colonel David Jablonsky

Editor
Mrs. Marianne P. Cowling

Secretary
Ms. Patricia A. Bonneau

******